If Jesus Had a Child

Dr. B. Glenn Wilkerson

CROSSLINK
PUBLISHING

If Jesus Had a Child

CrossLink Publishing
www.crosslinkpublishing.com

ISBN 978-1-936746-99-6

Library of Congress Control Number: 2014931043

T his book is lovingly dedicated to Karen, my amazing wife of forty-five years. She is as loving, brilliant, caring, and supportive a person as I have ever known. It is also dedicated to our four wonderful children: Kevin, Kelly, Shay, and Shanyn. They, along with their mother, have constituted my life's greatest joy.

And, finally, the book honors the memory
of our sweet infant son, Shane Ryan Wilkerson.

Contents

PART V

Jesus' Approach to Some Difficult Issues

Introduction

*I*f *Jesus Had a Child* provides a new, dynamic parenting focus based on spiritual principles taught through words and deeds by Jesus Christ. While Jesus never married or had children of His own, He was the best "people-person" who ever lived. This book examines "What would Jesus do if He had a child?" The concepts and principles are easy to understand and apply, and are just as relevant in relationships between adults as they are in relationships between parents and children.

The book's message is primarily conveyed through storytelling, because spinning stories is what I like to do best. The book provides practical advice on making kids resilient to peer pressure, bullying, teasing, violence, drugs and alcohol, eating disorders, and other issues faced by today's youth. It touches on topics such as "encouragement versus praise," "why punishment doesn't work," and "identifying the unmet needs that cause a child to misbehave." More importantly, it teaches the principles of unconditional love that create high self-esteem and a positive self-concept.

If the Bible is to be relevant to the present, it must be brought to a crossing point with the issues that currently occupy our lives. *If*

Jesus Had a Child combines Jesus' teachings with raising children as if He were walking the earth today. This book breaks new ground in pairing spiritual truth with modern research regarding parenting.

While the concepts described in this book constitute a research-driven, twenty-first-century parenting paradigm, they are a reflection of spiritual principles taught by Jesus over 2,000 years ago. God has revealed his unconditional love for each of us through Jesus Christ. The purpose of this book is to help parents learn how to be the hands, feet, and heart of the Christ in conveying that love to their children.

Jesus invited everyone to embrace their incredible, intrinsic worth as a child of God. Being a "child of God" means being loved, accepted, and forgiven in spite of our mistakes and imperfections. It is the definition Jesus would have given to the term "self-esteem." If Jesus had a child, He would create self-esteem in His child by loving him for who he *is* rather than for what he *does*. Great parenting begins with following Jesus' example.

The book gives practical examples of applying the concepts of unconditional love in everyday living. It examines the three basic categories of children's misbehavior—negative attention-seeking, rebellion, and power confrontations—and provides tools for recognizing and addressing those misbehaviors.

The concepts, principles, and techniques described in *If Jesus Had a Child* are for great parents who want to become even better at the most difficult, rewarding, and important job in the world. The book will also be invaluable for parents who have kids who are engaging in "at-risk" behaviors. Its simple yet profound message is for parents, grandparents, teachers, counselors, coaches, church workers, and all caring adults who want to prepare children for full-throttled participation in courageous, joy-filled living.

When Craig Reynolds was playing shortstop for the Houston Astros, a reporter approached him during the National League Conference Championship Series with the New York Mets and asked him how he handled the pressure. The reporter said, "Suppose it's the bottom of the ninth inning, last at bat, and your team is behind 1-0. There are two outs, with the bases loaded; and you're at the plate. You have a 3-2 count on you. The next pitch will decide the outcome of the game. If you get a hit, two runs score, and you're the hero. If you strike out, you're the goat. How do you deal with that sort of pressure?"

Craig said, "I know that when the game is over, I'm going to drive home to a family and to a church that are going to love me no matter what. Whether I get a hit or strike out won't alter how they feel about me. Knowing that they are going to love me—no matter what I do—allows me to step up to the plate, relax, and do the best that I can."

Craig Reynolds's words illustrate the tremendous spiritual and psychological strength conveyed by unconditional love and why it is a parent's greatest gift to a child. The most important aspect of parenting is nurturing our children and assuring them that they are loved without condition. It is what Jesus would do if He had a child!

Did Jesus Really Say That?

While I have notched over forty years in the ministry, I have not had a personal conversation with Jesus regarding the matters discussed in this book. However, based on my study of Jesus' life and teachings, the content reflects how I think Jesus would go about raising a child. In some instances, I have even ventured to "quote" Jesus, paraphrasing words and thoughts I think He might have in response to a given situation.

There are questions at the end of each chapter. I hope that those questions will be helpful in regard to your individual assimilation of the material. I also hope that they will be useful in stimulating group discussion on *If Jesus Had a Child*.

PART I

Jesus' Three Pillars of Great Parenting

Chapter 1

Pillar One: Providing Unconditional Love

Dear friends, since God so loved us, we also ought to love one another....We love because He first loved us (1 John 4:11, 19).

The most important need of a child is to feel loved. However, not just any kind of love will do. To be effective, it has to be a special kind of love called "unconditional love." Unconditional love is unearned love, and it is life-changing for children fortunate enough to receive it from a caring adult.

Years ago, a professor at Johns Hopkins University in Baltimore, Maryland, gave a group of graduate students an assignment. They were to go to the slums, select 200 boys between the ages of twelve and sixteen, investigate their backgrounds and environment, and then predict the kids' future. After interviewing the boys, gathering as much data as they could, and comparing it to social statistics, the students predicted that ninety percent of the boys would spend some time in jail.

Twenty-five years later, another group of graduate students at Johns Hopkins was given the job of testing the prediction. They went back to the slum area. Some of the boys—who were now men—still lived there. A few had died. But the students got in touch with 180 out of the original 200 kids. They found that only four of the group had ever been sent to jail.

Why was it that these men, who had been raised in a breeding ground of crime, had such a surprisingly good record? In the course of their interviews with the men, the researchers were constantly told, "Well, there was this teacher...." The researchers pressed further and discovered that in seventy-five percent of the cases, it was the same teacher.

The students located the teacher in a retirement home. They asked her how she had exerted such a remarkable influence over this group of former slum children. Could she give them any reasons why these men should have remembered her? She said, "No, I really can't." Then, as she thought back over the years, she said meditatively, more to herself than to the researchers, "I sure did love those boys...."

That teacher intuitively loved those young men. She loved them just as they came to her: loud, raunchy, caring, quiet, unkempt, self-centered, cool, and shy. She loved them for who they were—precious children of God—and her love and her faith in them prompted them to rise to her expectations. It is the job of every adult who interacts with children—especially those of us who are parents.

The Primary Job of a Parent

Virtually all parents love their children. The problem is that many children do not *feel* loved. The primary task of parenting is for adults to bridge this gap between reality and perception by learning how to give their children the unconditional love that allows them to embrace their worth as valued children of God.

It is important that we understand the nature of unconditional love. When we use the term, we are not talking about a mushy, sentimental emotion. Unconditional love means making a *conscious decision* to relate to children in a certain way. Unconditional love:

- separates the person from the behavior;
- loves a person for who she *is* rather than for what she *does*;
- is not permissive, but encourages responsibility.

Unconditional love does not shield a child from the consequences of her misbehavior. It requires, however, that those consequences be applied in a manner that never causes the child to doubt the love and affection of the parent. It means, for example, telling a teenager who has "borrowed" our car without our permission:

You are my child, and I love you. Furthermore, there's nothing you could ever do to keep me from loving you. There are consequences, however, when you misbehave. So, let's talk about what those consequences are for taking my car without asking me first....

Unconditional love distinguishes the person from her behavior and values the child for who she *is* rather than for what she *does*. When a child realizes that she is loved without condition, it empowers her to believe, "I am a person of real value in spite of my mistakes and shortcomings!" and she can be released from any unresolved feelings of shame or guilt.

One of the world's most effective delivery systems for unconditional love is the Christian faith. God, who knows of our flaws, still loves and accepts us as we are. And our spiritual proof of His unconditional acceptance and love is Jesus Christ upon a cross. Our highest endeavor as parents is to try, as best we can, to love our children in the same manner that God has loved us through the Christ.

How are we to love our children? Jesus instructed us to "love others as you love yourself,"[1] and here is the catch: loving a child as we love ourselves will not do that child much good *unless* we have a healthy love and appreciation of ourselves. And, for us to love ourselves, we must first feel loved by someone "greater" than ourselves. For a child, that someone is the parent. For an adult, that Someone is God.

To our rescue comes the Good News of the Gospel. Because God loved us first, we *are* able to love ourselves.[2] God's unconditional acceptance and love, conveyed through Jesus, allows us to value ourselves—and, in turn, to value our kids—as esteemed children of God.

In the vocabulary of Jesus, the definition of a *child of God* is "a person who is the recipient of God's unmerited forgiveness and love." It is the key element in a person's developing high self-esteem. Imparting to our children this Christian—and love-based—sense of self-esteem is a parent's most important task.

What Would Jesus Do?

For a period of time, pins and bracelets with the initials "WWJD" were popular among our young people. The adage "What Would Jesus Do?" may seem a little simplistic, but actually it is an excellent barometer for making everyday decisions regarding our engagement in quality living. While Jesus did not have children of His own, His guidelines for living and loving are a model for all relationships, including those between parents and their children. In every situation where a parent is faced with decisions regarding a basic philosophy of parenting—or how to respond to a specific behavior of a child—a good question to ask is: "What would Jesus do if He were parenting my child?"

Jesus did not leave us guessing in regard to His thoughts on parenting. He once told a story about a man who had two sons.[3]

One of the boys was impatient to leave his family and to experience life on his own. So he asked his father for his inheritance, took the money, and left town for some foreign travel. Too immature to know how to handle his newfound freedom, he went a little crazy with his father's money. He quickly soaked up a small fortune on alcohol, parties, and too-willing women. To make matters worse, the country was struck by a severe famine, and he suddenly found himself hungry, homeless, and all alone in a foreign land. Raised on a farm, he had some experience in taking care of animals, so he took a job as a slop hand on a pig farm. Finally, penniless and starving, he became so desperate that he decided to go back and hire himself out as a servant on his father's farm. So he launched out for home.

The boy had made an absolute mess of his young life. He had lost all his money, flaunted his family's values, and now was reduced to begging his father for a job. As he neared home, his sense of shame weighed upon him like a sack of rocks, and his steps became slower and slower. Stumbling along, head down, he rehearsed his speech: "Father, I have sinned against heaven and before you. I am no longer worthy to be called your son; treat me as one of your hired hands." Suddenly, he heard shouts, and, as he looked up, he saw a man running toward him. It was his father!

His father had seen him coming, and, sandals flapping, hair flying, his robe flared out behind him, he was sprinting down the road to welcome his boy home. With tears streaming down his cheeks, he swept his son into his arms and hugged and kissed him. Summoning the entire family, the father called for a celebration.

In Jesus' story, the son was not going to have to work his way back into his dad's good graces. His father had already made the decision to love and accept the boy no matter what he had done. It is *the* story of unconditional love, and it reveals the heart of Christ.

Jesus' message was that God loves us "no matter what." We are called to do the same with our children. It does not mean that we allow poor behavior; rather, we learn how to discipline the behavior while still valuing the worth of the child. This gift of unconditional love allows a young person to value himself in spite of his imperfections and is the key to high self-esteem and a positive self-concept.

New Research Confirms the Teachings of Jesus

Jesus brought Good News that can save us from the feelings of shame and guilt that can make this life a "hell on earth." He said that being a forgivable, lovable child of God is ours to claim. Feeling valued and esteemed as a human being is a matter of saying, "Yes!" to a relationship with God. Furthermore, as the Apostle Paul points out, this amazing love of God is not something we can earn through our achievements or "good works." It comes to us as God's free, unearned gift.

For many people, however, spiritual insights are not enough to convince them that something is true. They want factual evidence and scientific proof.

In cooperation with the University of Texas School of Public Health, the ARK*Group* conducted ground-breaking research that confirms the teachings of Jesus regarding how self-esteem is created in children. Three hundred and eight high school and middle school students in the Klein and Magnolia Independent School Districts (Texas) were surveyed in regard to what makes them feel good about themselves. The research demonstrated that "over the long haul," the single most important factor in a child's high self-esteem is for that child to receive unconditional love from a primary adult in that child's life.[4]

Contrary to popular belief, self-esteem (feeling valued as a child of God) is not created through achievements or high-octane performance. Instead, high self-esteem is the product of nurturing relationships and unconditional love.

This University of Texas study created a new paradigm in regard to how children can be taught to image themselves. A child's overall view of himself is his "self-concept," and his self-concept consists of two very distinct components: "self-worth" and "self-esteem." Self-worth has to do with the child's feeling valued on the basis of what he *does*. Self-esteem has to do with the child's feeling valued on the basis of who he *is*. In summary:

- **Self-concept** (the overall way in which a person views himself) is composed of two things: self-worth and self-esteem.
- **Self-worth** is the product of achievement and performance (being valued for what we *do*). The Apostle Paul called it "good works."
- **Self-esteem** is the product of unconditional love (being valued for who we *are*). Paul called it "grace."

Another critical discovery emanating from the University of Texas research is that self-esteem contributes two-thirds to a child's self-concept while self-worth contributes one-third. It is called the Self-Concept Triad.[5]

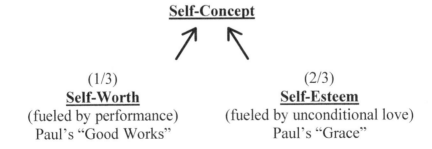

Self-Concept

(1/3)
Self-Worth
(fueled by performance)
Paul's "Good Works"

(2/3)
Self-Esteem
(fueled by unconditional love)
Paul's "Grace"

As important as it is to help a child achieve and perform, self-esteem (fueled by unconditional love) is twice as important as self-worth (fueled by performance) in its contribution to a child's concept of self.

Self-esteem and self-worth are different, and the importance of the distinction between the two cannot be overemphasized. A skilled, competent murderer sitting on death row could test high in regard to his feelings of self-worth but feel miserable about himself regarding his feelings of self-esteem. That is the reason why the old prison research often gave false readings regarding inmates' "self-esteem."[6, 7] The studies were actually measuring self-worth rather than self-esteem.

Some respected researchers in the past have debunked self-esteem, saying that it does not improve grades or facilitate career achievement. Again, those researchers were operating under the old definitions and were in actuality testing the impact of self-worth rather than self-esteem. The new definition of self-esteem separates the deed from the doer and emphasizes the value of the person rather than the person's performance.

Another point of contention raised by critics against the old self-esteem movement is that it turned a generation of adults into "praise junkies." If a child could stand up and breathe hard enough to fog a mirror, some parents or teachers would want to award that child a trophy or a ribbon. This misguided approach provokes disdain and derision from its critics—and rightfully so. Self-esteem is not bolstered by false praise. To the contrary, a healthy self-concept requires an accurate (and self-forgiving) appraisal of one's own gifts and abilities.

Still another popular misconception regarding self-esteem has been the tendency of some critics to equate egotism and self-centered arrogance with high self-esteem. The truth is that these "bravado traits" are actually a cover-up for feelings of low self-esteem. Audacity, conceit, arrogance, and narcissism (characterized by a false sense of superiority) are evidences of "pseudo" self-esteem. The reason why bullies and "tough guys" humiliate and put down others is because, inwardly, they do not feel good about themselves. They cut down others in hopes of making themselves feel important. When they take off their outer masks and allow us to peer into their souls, it is clear that such people are in desperate need of true self-esteem.

This profound difference between self-worth and self-esteem explains a person like Mike Tyson. What a dichotomy! On the one hand, Mike was one of the greatest boxing champions of all time. In his prime, he was a peerless performer in the ring—the youngest man ever to hold the world heavyweight title. It is no wonder a high achiever like Mike would have a big ego and strong feelings of self-worth.

But there is another side to Mike Tyson's life. While he was never knocked out in boxing, he lost consciousness several times as a result of beatings he received as a child. Raised in a troubled home, he grew up feeling unwanted and unloved—which is a formula for the development of low self-esteem. He bullied men, abused women, and was eventually convicted of rape. Even while in prison, he seemed outwardly cocky and full of pride, but it was all an outer sham. Inwardly, he has been burdened with feelings of sadness, hopelessness, and helplessness all his life.[8]

In perhaps one of the saddest interviews ever aired on television, Mike said, "Maybe in my next life, I'll have a better life. And that's why I'm just looking forward to go to the other world. 'Cause I really hate the way I live now."[9] Understanding the difference between self-esteem and self-worth helps us make sense out of Mike Tyson's self-assessment: "I have no self-esteem but the biggest ego in the world."[10]

The new research confirms that a healthy self-concept depends upon high self-esteem, and high self-esteem is created through relationships of unconditional love. What we have observed to be true for the past 2,000 years has been validated by scientific study. Jesus must be smiling.

The Implications of the New Research

The old self-esteem movement (circa 1970s–1990s) mistakenly embraced and promoted a false premise. The mantra was, "If parents can help a child to discover her unique strengths and then enable her to actualize her potential in regard to those strengths, she'll feel good about herself."

The problem with this line of thinking is that many high achievers are actually driven by a sense of low self-esteem. We see it all around us—men and women who think, "If I could just get a better car...or a bigger house...or another promotion at work, maybe I would finally feel good about myself." Tragically, our kids are often subjected to that same performance pressure as a means of valuing themselves.

I was raised in a west Texas town called Odessa, where football is valued right next to religion in terms of importance. When I was growing up, my friends and I came to believe that to be male and to have worth meant playing football. But just making the team was not enough. Then, it became a matter of:

if I could just earn a letter...
if I could just make the starting lineup...
if I could make All-City...
if I could make All-District...
if I could make All-State...
then I might feel good about myself.

I noticed an unexpected thing, though. A week after the honors had been announced in the local newspaper, the All-District and All-

State performers on our team did not seem to feel any better about themselves than did the rest of us.

Life contains a lot of bad news for folks who stake their worth on their achievements, because if the motivation for performing well is to feel good about ourselves, it just never quite happens for us. We are always "one achievement shy" of feeling fulfilled. That is why many of the world's greatest achievers have died feeling that their lives were a total waste. While achievement and performance do play an important role in the development of a person's self-concept, too much performance pressure can actually diminish a person's positive concept of self.

Often, even good parents lose their perspective when it comes to loving our children. We think that to show love, we have to prepare them to be winners—not just in one or two endeavors, but in everything. And so we apply the pressure—urging our young people to surge to the top academically, athletically, socially, and in all other extracurricular activities into which we dutifully push them.

We mean well, thinking it is a way of showing our children that we care about them. The trouble is that sort of love often ends up coming across as being extremely conditional, and children start feeling that we approve of them only when they win and excel. While kids need to know that we have high expectations of them, we walk a fine line with the emphasis we place upon their performance. There can come a point where we step over that line—then the more a child feels pushed, the more she feels unloved.

Years ago, there was an epidemic of teenage suicides in Plano, Texas. Over an eighteen-month period, nine teenagers took their own lives. Plano is one of those suburban communities where well-meaning parents push their kids on the fields of football, academics, cheerleading, and you-name-it to excel and be "number one." What went wrong for these children? When *60 Minutes* did a special on the Plano tragedy, the producers of the show came to the conclusion that the primary cause of the suicides was the "performance pressure placed upon these young people by adults." They felt like they could not live up to the expectations of their parents and the community in which they lived.

The children in Plano were being pushed by decent, caring, well-intentioned parents to succeed—to "be the best." And because the kids felt valued primarily for their achievements, some of them simply cracked under the pressure. While it is good to encourage their efforts, young people have a desperate need to feel loved for who they are rather than for how well they perform.

The new self-concept research—with its distinction between self-worth and self-esteem—dispels the misconceptions of the past. We now know that self-esteem is not the product of a person's performance. It has nothing to do with false praise. And it is not evidenced by arrogant, conceited behavior (which is actually a cover for low self-esteem). Self-esteem means feeling loved for who you are rather than for what you do, and it is the product of unconditional love.

And those who are really good at working with children know the importance of emphasizing self-esteem over self-worth as a means of enhancing a child's overall concept of self.

Joe Ehrmann, a former star in the National Football League, was the volunteer coach of the Gilman Greyhounds, a high school football team in Baltimore, Maryland. Joe had a question-and-answer sequence he shares with his players.

Joe asks, "What is our job as coaches?"

The boys yell back in unison, "To love us."

Joe shoots back, "What is your job?"

The boys respond, "To love each other."

In 2001, the Greyhounds were the top-ranked team in the state of Maryland. They frequently are a ranked team in the national high school football polls. And yet, while they like to win, their coaches know that it is more important that their players feel valued for who they are rather than for their success on the field.[11]

When we combine the new research with the teachings of Jesus—and apply those principles in our everyday interactions with our children—we are on our way to becoming great coaches, great teachers, and great parents.

Understanding What Our Kids Need

This question was asked at a Houston leadership conference: "What are we going to do about the rising incidences of teenage violence in our city?" A streetwise pastor replied:

> Whether they were raised in affluent neighborhoods or inner-city ghettoes, many of our young people today basically feel like no one cares about them. If you think that nobody cares about you, then you don't care about yourself. And kids who don't care about themselves had just as soon as take a gun and shoot someone as to look at them.
>
> We can't build enough prisons to house these children. The only answer to the anger and the violence being perpetrated by our young people in America today is for all of us "busy" adults to become more intentional about making them feel cherished and loved.[12]

In other words, if we are to help our children to value other people and other people's property, we must first help them to value themselves. And for them to love themselves, they must feel loved by adults who are significant in their lives.

A few years ago, a thirteen-year-old boy in Northeast Houston poured gasoline over an eleven-year-old boy and set him on fire. It was not an isolated affair. All over the nation, there have been incidents where children have taken guns and shot their parents and their classmates. These children are angry—violently angry. And they are angry because, for whatever reason, they do not feel loved. They feel abandoned, emotionally if not physically, and they feel hurt. And when we feel unloved and unlovely, we rage against those around us— treating others in precisely the same way we feel about ourselves.

That thirteen-year-old boy had been handed off from relative to relative. He did not have a mother or a father to offer him the unconditional love that would have allowed him to love himself. And not loving himself, he was cruel to those around him. The practical implications are clear. Unless we give our children unconditional love, our children will not value themselves and will be unable to claim their identity as children of God.

It is an issue of incredible importance. Young people who are engaged in drug and alcohol abuse, promiscuous sex, violence, and gang activity all suffer from low self-esteem. It takes a lot of ego-strength for a young person to retain his values in the face of negative peer pressure. And children who do not have a strong self-concept are terribly at-risk. Juvenile justice authorities now realize that aberrant juvenile behavior is almost always perpetrated by young people with low self-esteem who "cave in" to negative peer pressure in hopes of being "accepted." When they esteem themselves, children develop the inner strength to withstand the negative peer pressure that leads to antisocial and self-destructive behavior. The most important job of parents, teachers, and all caring adults is to provide kids unconditional love—the basic building block of high self-esteem.

There is a story about a high school boy who decided to try out for the football team. It was Monday, and the tryouts were to be held that day after classes. Before leaving for school that morning, he told his mother—a single, working mom—what he was going to do. All day, the boy felt nervous and apprehensive. He tried his best during the tryout, and, to his delight, he made the team.

The boy arrived home to a beautiful table set with the family's best china. His mother had prepared a marvelous meal. Immediately, he figured that one of his buddies had called on his cell phone and tipped her off. Finding his mother in the kitchen, he told her the good news. They hugged and then sat down to a wonderful meal. Next to his plate, the boy found a note. It read: "Congratulations, son! I appreciate your courage and your hard work in achieving your goal. This meal will tell you how much I love you."

While on his way to the kitchen to get some dessert, he noticed that a second card had fallen from her pocket. Picking it off the floor, he read: "Don't worry about not making the team. You are a wonderful young man whether you play football or not. I am proud of your efforts. This meal will tell you how much I love you."

Total acceptance! Total love! The mother's affection for her son was not contingent upon his success in football. In fact, just the opposite was true. If he had performed poorly or had been rejected by his coach, he would be all the more accepted at home. She stood behind him no matter what—softening the blows, healing the wounds, believing in him, and loving him. It is called unconditional love, and it means separating the person from the behavior and loving a person for who he is rather than for what he produces and achieves. Every child deserves that sort of love. It is the basis of true self-esteem. It is how Jesus would relate to a child.

If Jesus Had a Child...

Jesus said, "This is my commandment, that you love one another as I have loved you."[13] On the cross, he showed us that God loves and values us for who we *are*, not for what we *do*. The world tries to counter that by saying, "Don't you believe it! You must prove your worth through your achievements." And so, for many of us, the tragedy of our lives is that we waste them trying to show that we are winners and that we *deserve* to be respected and loved. A further tragedy is that, in our society, a lot of us try to be big winners vicariously through our children.

I wish I could take back some of those times when I was coaching my kids in football, softball, soccer, and baseball. Most of the time, I was pretty good about seeing the games for what they were: as an opportunity to be with children and to love on them and to teach them some things about sportsmanship, and that they can still be winners even when they lose. But there were a couple of instances where I would give anything for a do-over, times when I lost my head and pushed and criticized and made my own kids cry. And, looking back, I see that a lot of it was because I wanted them to excel so that I could bask in their reflected glory. Those of us who want to love our children—as Jesus loved us—need to monitor our behavior at our kids' activities.

In a peewee soccer game, the coach called one of his eight-year-old players aside and asked, "Do you understand what cooperation is? What a team is?" The little boy nodded yes. The coach said, "Do you understand that what matters is not whether we win or lose but how well we play together as a team?" The kid nodded yes again. "So," the coach continued, "when a foul is called, you shouldn't argue, curse, attack the referee, or call him a 'dumb horse's rear end.' Do you understand all that?" Again, the little boy nodded. The coach continued, "And when I take you out of the game so that another kid gets a chance to play, it's not good sportsmanship to call the coach 'a stupid jerk,' is it?" Again, the little boy nodded. "Good," said the coach. "Now go over there, and explain all that to your mother."

Parents, forget about all the pressure, the amount of playing time, and all the other stuff that ruins peewee sports for us and the kids. All that craziness about athletic scholarships and trophies—when all is said and done—those things mean nothing. What really matters are our relationships with our children.

When she was nineteen years old, the famous Swiss-born psychiatrist Elisabeth Kubler-Ross volunteered to help rebuild villages in Europe that had been destroyed by World War II. Her experiences with people in postwar Germany, many of whom had known Hitler as a child, led her to conclude:

> If I had been mistreated like Hitler was as a child, who knows how I would have turned out?…We need to understand why Hitler was capable of doing what he did. He was terribly abused and traumatized as a child. If he had been given halfway decent love as a child instead of being constantly hurt and traumatized…he wouldn't have destroyed millions of people.[14]

Kubler-Ross said, "If we could give one generation of children unconditional love, there would be no Hitlers."

Unconditional love generates the self-esteem that generates the self-concept that generates a young person's realization that he or she is a unique, beloved child of God. If Jesus had a child, He would provide that love. It is the first pillar of great parenting.

[1] Mark 12:31, NRSV.

[2] 1John 4:19.

[3] Luke 15: 11–24.

[4] Dr. Ron Lorimar, "The New Research Linking Unconditional Love with High Self-Esteem and a Positive Self-Concept," The University of Texas School of Public Health, August 1994.

[5] Lorimar.

[6] Erica Goode, "Deflating Self-Esteem's Role in Society's Ills," *The New York Times*, Health Section, October 1, 2002.

[7] Lauren Slater, "The Trouble with Self-Esteem," *The New York Times,* Magazine Desk, February 3, 2002.

[8] *Houston Chronicle*, 10/14/97, Sec. B, p. 3.

[9] Mike Tyson on Fox Sports Net's "Beyond the Glory."

[10] *Houston Chronicle,* 10/14/97, Sec. B, p. 3.

[11] Jeffrey Marx, *The Season of Life*, August 29, 2004.

[12] Pastor Kirbyjon Caldwell, Mayor's Conference on Teen Violence, Houston, Texas, February 2002.

[13] John 15:12, NRSV.

[14] *Parade Magazine*, August 11, 1991, p. 12.

Discussion Ideas

- What was the primary type of love you received from your parents? Was it conditional or unconditional? Give some examples.

- As an adult, have you ever been in a situation where you felt like you were only appreciated and liked for what you did, or achieved, rather than for who you are? Describe your feelings.

- What has been your greatest emphasis in raising your child: preparing him for a successful life or celebrating him for who he is? Do you feel a need to change your emphasis?

- Will giving your child unconditional love require a change from the way in which you were parented in your home of origin? If so, explain what you intend to do differently.

Chapter 2

Pillar Two: Inspiring a Servant's Heart

After six days Jesus took with him Peter, James and John the brother of James, and led them up a high mountain by themselves. There he was transfigured before them. His face shone like the sun, and his clothes became as white as the light. Just then there appeared before them Moses and Elijah, talking with Jesus. Peter said to Jesus, "Lord, it is good for us to be here. If you wish, I will put up three shelters—one for you, one for Moses and one for Elijah." While he was still speaking, a bright cloud covered them, and a voice from the cloud said, "This is my Son, whom I love; with him I am well pleased. Listen to him!" When the disciples heard this, they fell facedown to the ground, terrified. But Jesus came and touched them. "Get up," he said. "Don't be afraid." When they looked up, they saw no one except Jesus.

As they were coming down the mountain, Jesus instructed them, "Don't tell anyone what you have seen, until the Son of Man has been raised from the dead."...When they came to the crowd, a man approached Jesus and knelt before him. "Lord, have mercy on my son," he said. "He has seizures and is suffering greatly. He often falls into the fire or into the water...." Jesus rebuked the demon, and it came out of the boy, and he was healed at that moment (Matthew 17:1–9, 14–16, 18).

J esus would teach His child to have faith. He would encourage His child to accept the spiritual truth that she is a child of God—loved and accepted by Him "no matter what you do." That's one aspect of the faith journey: personal spiritual growth. The second part of the faith journey—and equally important—is to share that love with others.

Matthew tells the story of Jesus' taking Peter, James, and John and leading them up a high mountain by themselves. While they were up there, Jesus underwent some sort of spiritual transformation whereby his face appeared to shine like the sun. It was one of those spiritual mountaintop experiences, and it was so special that Peter said, "I say we stay!" and he proposed building houses on top of the mountain.

What took place next was very, very symbolic. Instead of allowing everybody to stay up on a spiritual mountaintop and isolate themselves in their newfound spirituality, Jesus led them back down the mountain and into a crowd of people who were waiting for them. And the first thing he did upon his return was to talk to a father who had an epileptic son—a boy who was suffering terribly from the disease—and Jesus healed the boy.[1] What Jesus did that day was to model the sort of balance that characterizes great faith—engaging in personal spiritual growth *and* helping those who are in need.

Jesus literally instructed His followers to minister to those who are poor, thirsty, hungry, lonely, sick, and incarcerated. He said, "Just as you did it to one of the least of these who are members of my family, you did it to me."[2] The good news in regard to our children is that they willingly accept this charge. Children innately want to help others.

A few years ago, at the Seattle Special Olympics, nine contestants, all physically or mentally disabled, assembled at the starting line for the 100-yard dash. At the sound of the gun, they all started out, not exactly in a dash, but with a desire to run the race to the finish and win.

All, that is, except one little boy who stumbled on the asphalt, tumbled over a couple of times and began to cry. The other eight heard the boy cry. They slowed down and looked back. Then they all turned around and went back—every one of them.

One girl with Down's syndrome bent down and kissed him and said: "This will make it better." Then all nine linked arms and walked together to the finish line. Everyone in the stadium stood, and the cheering went on for several minutes. People who were there were thrilled by the spectacle. Why? Because, deep down, we know this one thing: *what matters in this life is helping others even if it means slowing down and changing our course.* Life's most profound meaning involves reaching out to people, locking arms, and helping each other to finish the race together.

When they are given opportunities to serve others and make life better for them, children are given a sense of purpose and meaning. That's why "inspiring a 'servant's heart'" is the second pillar of great parenting.

In working with His child, Jesus would share the great teachings of faith regarding God's unconditional love; but He would not allow His daughter to just sit and listen. He would also provide situations where she could "act out" those teachings so that not only her mind but also her heart could understand them.

If parents intentionally look, opportunities to serve and help others abound around us, although sometimes it takes a little creativity to see them. An example of putting faith—and love—into practice is this anecdotal story of Fiorello La Guardia:

On a blustery cold winter night in 1935, La Guardia, the five-foot-four-inch mayor of New York City, strode into a courtroom and gave the judge the night off. That sort of behavior was characteristic of

Mayor La Guardia. He had a good eye for spotting people who could use a little help.

On this particular night, La Guardia walked into a courtroom in one of the toughest parts of the city and said to the judge, "You've been working hard. Take the night off. I'll handle your cases." He mounted the bench and asked for the first case. An older woman in a torn, tattered coat was brought before him. He asked, "What's the charge?" and was told, "Your honor, she's charged with stealing a loaf of bread."

"Did you do it?" the mayor asked.

"Yes," the old woman replied. "I'm guilty. I admit it. I stole the loaf of bread."

La Guardia inquired, "Why? Why would you steal a loaf of bread?"

She said, "Mr. Mayor, my daughter and her husband have two beautiful children. But my son-in-law recently deserted the family. So, my poor daughter is trying to raise the two girls on her own, and she's out of work. Now she's sick, and she can't get hospitalization. I went through her house the other day trying to find food, and there was nothing for them to eat. I have very little money myself. So I stole the bread. But, Mr. Mayor, I can't afford a fine, and I can't afford to be put in jail."

"Just a minute!" the grocery store owner called out. "I'm the one who brought the charges against this woman. I've heard sob stories like this before, but justice has to be done. This is one of the toughest sections of New York, and, if you let her off for stealing bread, there's not going to be any justice in this city."

Mayor La Guardia thought for a moment. Of course, the grocery store owner was right. He looked at the woman and said, "You're guilty! Ten dollars or ten days in jail!"

The old woman began to weep. Mayor La Guardia reached into his back pocket and took out his wallet. He extracted a ten-dollar bill and put it in his famous top hat that he had laid beside the bench. Then he said, "You're guilty. You owe ten dollars, but your debt has been paid."

And with that, La Guardia handed his hat to the bailiff and said, "Mr. Bailiff, pass my hat around the courtroom. I'm fining everyone in this courtroom fifty cents for living in a city where a grandmother would have to steal bread to feed her grandchildren."

The next day, the *New York Times* reported that a bewildered woman was handed $47.50 by the bailiff, 50 cents of which was contributed by the red-faced grocery store owner who had brought the poor woman to court. Almost $40 was contributed by the people in that courtroom—police officers, the bailiff, and other petty criminals awaiting their trials—all of whom, having paid 50 cents, rose and gave Mayor La Guardia a standing ovation. The *New York Times* said, "It was an extraordinary moment of grace."[3]

If faith is to be truly understood, we must first *hear* the great words of faith and allow them to take root in us. Then we must *live* that faith through the everyday events of our lives—so that it not only speaks to our heads but speaks to our hearts as well.

A great example of a person allowing his faith to inform his actions is the late Dr. Martin Luther King Jr. One of the great Christian reformers of the twentieth century, King used the tactic of "passive resistance" to combat the evil of racism in America. Inspired by Jesus' teachings regarding loving our enemies and "turning the other cheek" when accosted by those who hated him, King was beaten, pummeled with powerful water hoses wielded by law enforcement officials, and put in county jails. Yet, refusing to strike back physically, he continued to lead peaceful marches protesting racial discrimination. And, in the end, love prevailed. Martin's leadership helped bring about the Civil Rights Act of 1964, a pivotal piece of legislation that transformed the status of black people and other minorities in America.

While Martin Luther King Jr. provides a dramatic example of the two-edged nature of faith, there are thousands of similar but unpublicized acts of courage that take place around us every day. Living one's faith most often does take courage, because it means standing against the forces of evil, greed, and indifference that torment the lives of the poor, the aged, and the weak. Jesus' opponents constantly criticized Him for spending time with, and helping, people who were sick or whose life circumstances forced them into prostitution or who were being exploited by the economic powers of His time. And He did not just rush to the aid of the poor; He addressed the spiritual poverty of many who were rich and powerful but whose lives were lonely and meaningless. The love that God invested in Him Jesus poured into the loves of those around Him.

While children have a need to serve, that basic human need likely will not be fulfilled without the help of an intentional adult. Children should be given the opportunity to visit homeless shelters, food pantries, homes for the elderly and disabled, and other places where they can be encouraged to serve others—where they can see their parent and other respected adults model a "servant's heart."

Jesus would teach His child to develop a rich inner life of the Spirit and then to translate faith into action by helping the sick, the hungry, the elderly, and the poor. It is not either-or; it is a case of both. In fact, one leads to the other, and, practiced together, they form the core experiences out of which life's most profound meaning is to be extracted. After the mountaintop spiritual experience, people of faith must follow Jesus down the mountain, enter the crowd, and offer solace and comfort to those in need. That is the life of faith that Jesus would model for His child.

[1] Matthew 17:1–9, 14–16, 18.
[2] Matthew 25:40.
[3] Brennan Manning, *The Ragamuffin Gospel*, 2000.

Discussion Ideas

- Is there a person in your life who has modeled a "servant's heart"? Who? How was it expressed?
- Do you agree that a single-minded search for "personal spiritual growth" is only one-half of the Gospel? Explain your thoughts.
- How do you translate God's love into personal action?
- What activities could be considered to instill compassion for others in your child?

Chapter 3

Pillar Three: Liberating Ourselves from the Past

Therefore, if anyone is in Christ, he is a new creation; the old has gone, the new has come! All this is from God, who reconciled us to Himself through Christ and gave us the ministry of reconciliation (2 Corinthians 5: 17–18).

There is a story involving a newlywed husband who was watching his wife prepare a pot roast. As he watched, she cut off one end of what looked like a perfectly good roast and threw it away. When he asked her why, she said, "Because my mother always did it that way!"

The man was confused. So he went to his mother-in-law and asked her why she always cut off the end of the roast before cooking it. She said, "Because *my* mother always did it that way!"

At the next family gathering, the man went to his wife's grandmother, now eighty years old, and asked her about this strange family practice. The old woman laughed. She said, "I don't know why my daughter and my granddaughter do it, but I always cut off the end of a pot roast because my pan was too small."

It takes courage and insight for us to question the traditions and practices that have been in our families for generations and to free ourselves from those behaviors that no longer make sense or, in some cases, even cause harm or stress. That is especially true of parenting behaviors.

Can you remember when you were growing up and an incident took place between you and your parents, and you said to yourself, "I'll *never* treat my kids like that"? Yet we tend to repeat our parents' behaviors in dealing with our own children. The ways that people parent their children are passed on from generation to generation. It takes a lot of effort to break the pattern.

Jesus calls us to examine the parenting behaviors we received as children—with the intent of passing on those parenting techniques that helped us feel loved while getting rid of those techniques that made us feel bad about ourselves. In this way, new and improved parenting skills can be introduced into our families that will be handed down to our children and to our children's children.

For us to break away from some of the ways in which our parents parented us and to create new ways of relating to each other as members of a family, we must take the final step toward becoming independent adults—which means learning to parent ourselves. It is a step that most of us do not take until we are in our twenties and thirties. It means taking full responsibility for our actions and having the courage, whenever appropriate, to chart new paths that are different from what our parents passed on to us. For many people, it is one of the most difficult things they will ever do.

The final step to adulthood—the key to our becoming emotionally mature—lies in our acceptance of the fact that our parents either totally *do* accept and approve of us or they *do not*. If parental acceptance is unconditional, we do not have to do a thing to earn it. Whatever we do, our parents will still approve of us and love us. On the other hand, if parental acceptance is conditional, *there is nothing we can ever do to earn it.* Everything we do in hopes of winning parental approval will never be quite good enough.

It is a tragic phenomenon. Sometimes, people fifty and sixty years of age will still be trying to win the approval of parents long since dead and gone, driven by parental demands for excellence that still echo in their minds. If any of us find ourselves constantly placed in a position where we feel we must earn parental love and approval, the only thing to be done is to recognize the futility of our efforts and to quit playing the game.

The most effective means of liberating ourselves from the past is to recognize and forgive our parents' limitations. If the majority of the love we received from our parents was conditional in nature, in all likelihood, the reason they loved the way they did was because that is the kind of love they received from *their* parents. If it was conditional, then they, too, were never quite able to measure up. When your mother proudly brought home that first report card of *A*'s and *B*'s, her parents said, "*B*'s are not acceptable. We expect to see straight *A*'s on your next report card." Those who were never able to sufficiently match the expectations of their parents usually have trouble giving total approval to their own kids.

It is a game that can be played between parents and their children throughout their lifetimes. Then it is passed on to the next generation. Understanding this phenomenon allows us to free ourselves from it. Rather than blame our parents for the conditional love they gave us, we can forgive them and move on. After all, they loved us the best that they knew how to love.

A friend shared this story:

My father was a lawyer and wanted me to follow in his footsteps. When I was in high school, he and my mother let me know that they would be very disappointed if I did not become a lawyer. They both died in a car crash when I was a junior in college. Wanting to honor their wishes, I went to law school, got a law degree, and became a criminal defense attorney. I was successful and made a lot of money, just as my parents had hoped. But what I really wanted to do was to be a teacher. So, at age thirty-eight, I went back to school and got my teacher certification. I now teach middle school math and am the happiest I've been in my entire life.

This experience taught me to encourage my own son to pursue whatever career he decides he wants to do.

The prophet Ezekiel said that the sins of the father are not passed on to the son.[1] It means we are not responsible for our parents' behaviors, and, if we choose to do so, we can cut those behaviors out of our own lives. Those words give us permission to discard any detrimental parenting behaviors we might have received at the hands of our parent. As one man said, "My grandfather verbally and emotionally abused my father, and my father verbally and emotionally abused me. I guess I'm the first one in my family to recognize the chain of abuse. Those behaviors will stop with me."

Jesus said, "No one puts new wine into old wineskins. For the old skins would burst from the pressure."[2] New concepts of parenting will not fit into some of the old parenting behaviors practiced by our parents and by their parents before them. Jesus invites us to take an objective look at the parenting techniques employed by our parents— keeping those behaviors that were love-based and uplifting while discarding those that were fear-based and punitive.

It is a liberating experience to understand that we can break a cycle of conditional parenting and do things differently with our own child. We can institute a new cycle of parenting behaviors—giving our children the unconditional acceptance and love that will be passed on to their children and their children's children. It is a gift that will enrich our families for generations to come.

[1]   Ezekiel 18:20.
[2]   Matthew 9:17.

Discussion Ideas

- What expectations of your parents are still driving forces in your life?

- What expectations of your parents have you chosen to discard?

- Share a parenting behavior you received from your parents that you *do* want to pass on to your children.

- Ezekiel said that a child is not responsible for—and does not have to repeat—the sins of his father. Share a parenting behavior received from your parent that you *do not* want to pass on to your child.

PART II

Jesus' Four Gifts

(That He Would Share with His Child)

Chapter 4

Love (Instead of Apathy)

If anyone says, "I love God," yet hates his brother, he is a liar. For anyone who does not love his brother, whom he has seen, cannot love God, whom he has not seen. And he has given us this command: Whoever loves God must also love his brother (1 John 4:20–21).

Malcolm Muggeridge once said that the worst disease is not cancer or leprosy. He said, "The worst disease in the whole world is being unloved, uncared for, and unwanted." *We need to feel wanted and loved.* When the people from whom we can rightfully expect to give us love seem apathetic toward us, it is literally spirit-killing. Giving God's unconditional love to our children—and allowing them to feel valued and esteemed—is a parent's greatest gift to a child.

Most parents love their children with all their heart. The problem lies in the fact that so many parents do not know *how* to convey that love, and, as a result, their children do not *feel* loved. The biggest challenge for the nurturing parent is learning how to convey unconditional love.

Saying "I Love You"

For starters, if we are going to give unconditional love to our kids, we must verbalize it. We have to *say* the words, "I love you." However, if our parents were not in the habit of saying "I love you" to us, then it is usually hard for us to say it to our kids, or, for that matter, even to our spouses.

I was raised in a family that was very demonstrative in our expressions of love. My father was a large, ex-professional football player with a heart of gold. Every night at bedtime, Daddy would grab each one of us four Wilkerson kids, give us a peck on the lips, hug us, tell us he loved us, and send us off to bed. Mother would do the same. That is how we were raised, and, to this day, when my adult brothers and my sister see each other, we always greet with a hug and a kiss.

My wife, on the other hand, was raised in a family where there was love, but it was not expressed overtly. They did not say, "I love you," and they did not touch. For the first two years of our marriage, when we would have a telephone conversation with my folks, I would always end it by saying, "I sure do love you!" and they would always reply, "We sure do love you, too." For the first two years of our marriage, whenever we would have a telephone conversation with my wife's parents, I would always end it by saying, "I love you," and the best they could do for the first two years was to reply, "Us, too."

But here is the good news: within five years, it all changed. When we got together with my in-laws, her father started giving me a peck on the lips, hugging me, and saying, "I sure do love you." Her mother still could not quite countenance the lip-pecking, so she would give me a kiss on the cheek, hug me, and tell me she loved me.

It is a learned behavior. Regardless of what we experienced in our homes of origin, we can start today by telling our kids, "I love you." If we are going to give unconditional love to our child, we must begin by saying it. Children's hearts hunger for these words, and they need to hear them every day.

We also should be alert to other opportunities to affirm our children verbally. Encouraging words such as, "You really put yourself into this project," "I'm glad you are my child," "I know you'll make the right decision," and "You're really fun to be with," are important. Comments like these may seem insignificant at the time, but they nurture the relationship between us and our children.

However, for our words to have meaning, our *behavior* must also show unconditional love to our children. In fact, our actions are even more important than our words. Here are four ways of showing unconditional love to our child through our actions:

Dr. B. Glenn Wilkerson

Physical Touch

One powerful means of conveying love is through physical touch. Jesus made it a point to touch children as a means of showing His love for them.[1]

Children have an incredible need for the loving touch of nurturing adults (especially their parents!). In the 1990s, the world was outraged to learn of the conditions in state-run orphanages in Romania. An estimated 170,000 children were housed in these mass orphanages.[2] Scores of babies would be placed in cribs in a single room, with only a couple of nurses assigned to take care of them. The nurses were so overworked that the best they could do would be to change diapers a couple of times a day and to pop a bottle in each child's mouth two or three times a day. The babies were not picked up or held. As a result, the children suffered from what came to be known as the "failure to thrive" syndrome.[3] Because of the lack of a warm human touch, many of the babies became emotionally traumatized and stunted; some of them even died. We are built to be touched and held and nurtured. And when that nurturing does not take place, we spiritually, physically, and emotionally die.

The need to be touched in positive ways is as real and necessary as the need for air and water. Touching may take a variety of forms—from playful wrestling or a pat on the back to hugging and kissing. A loving, caring physical touch confirms a child's sense of being loved.

Parenting behaviors are passed within a family from generation to generation, usually without question, until someone has the insight to introduce new patterns of behavior into the parenting chain. If our own parents were not in the habit of saying, "I love you," or of touching us in loving, affirming ways, it will probably be difficult for us to do so with our children. It is important that we have the wisdom and the courage to begin blessing our children (and therefore our children's children) with these new behaviors.

Eye Contact

Eye contact is an important element in the giving of parental love. In his book *How to Really Love Your Child*, Dr. Ross Campbell says:

Without realizing it, we use eye contact as a primary means of conveying love, especially to a child. A child uses eye contact with his parents (and others) to feed emotionally.... After a child is approximately six to eight weeks of age, you will notice that his eyes are always moving and seem to be searching for something. The eyes resemble two radar antennae constantly moving and searching. Do you know what he's looking for? I think you already know; he's searching for another set of eyes.[4]

Lovers instinctively know the importance of eye contact in conveying feelings of love. On a dinner date, they will gaze lovingly at each other across the table. And what is true for adults is even truer in regard to the needs of a child.

Instead of watching television and at the same time trying to carry on a conversation with our child, we should either say, "Please give me fifteen minutes to finish watching this program, and then we'll talk," or we should turn off the television immediately and establish eye contact. "Giving our eyes" to our child is a primary means of giving unconditional love.

Individual Attention

Another technique for showing love involves the gift of our time: giving our child some individual attention. This means giving a child full, undivided attention—the sort of attention that allows a child to feel special and important. The giving of personal attention is a wonderful gift, for time is usually a parent's most scarce and most valued possession.

In many two-parent families, both parties work to maintain the lifestyle. Then there are a lot of single-parent families where the parent is really stretched to put in the necessary hours at work and still have time to engage with his or her children. Add in all the adult social and recreational stuff, and what happens? We get busy and run out of time to be with them, and we beg off with the excuse that the time we do spend with our kids is "quality" time. Our kids need *quantity* as well as *quality* time. Psychologists say that our children need fifteen minutes of individual time with their parent every day. Most kids are lucky to get fifteen minutes of individual time with their parent a week. So, we try to ease our consciences by buying them off with trinkets and money. Kids do not need more money. They need us to "be there" for them.

And, in addition to giving them individual attention, "being there" for our children also includes attending their activities. A lot of times, children will inform their parents about some event in which they are participating and then say, "It's no big deal. You don't need to bother coming." Never trust those words. Our kids do not mean them.

Our daughter Kelly played high school soccer. Her senior year, the last game of the season was Parents' Night. At halftime, all the girls gathered at midfield with their parents. And, as their names were announced on the public address system, each girl—with her parents on her arms—would walk toward the stands to the applause of the crowd. So, when it came Kelly's turn, the announcer said, "Kelly Wilkerson is being escorted by her parents, Glenn and Karen Wilkerson." Did you know that over half of the girls did not have a parent show up that night, and we had to recruit surrogate parents out of the stands to escort the girls from midfield to the sidelines?

After I got through escorting Kelly, I returned to midfield twice to escort two other girls. As we were walking toward the sidelines, the announcer would say, "Tonight, Rhea Johnson is escorted by her friend, Dr. Glenn Wilkerson." Each time, I would glance over out of the corner of my eye and see the girl crying. Now, many of those girls drove themselves to the game in fine cars—cars at least as expensive, if not more so, than the ones their parents drive. But their parents did not show up for Parents' Night!

We cannot substitute trinkets as an adequate replacement for meaningful time with our kids. Our children will not accept it. The school play, the band concert, athletic events, the dance recital, whatever our kids are doing—"being there" and supporting our children with our presence is a primary way of paying attention to our children and showing them that we love them.

There is a new social phenomenon that presents a real problem for many children today in regard to their parents' "being there" for them. A recent survey reveals that around forty percent of American children are born into single-parent families.[5] Who is going to be there as a male caregiver for kids whose fathers are nonexistent in their lives? At church, we men need to talk with our pastors and our youth ministers and ask if there are kids with absentee dads who need some attention from a caring male.

Jesus is our model for giving people individual attention. Time and again, He directed His personal attention to individuals, such as the two blind men outside of Jericho, whom nobody else had time for.[6] In spite of His disciples' efforts to hush the men and to rush Jesus past them, He stopped and ministered to the men and gave them His individual, undivided attention.

Empathy

Another expression of unconditional love is the gift of empathy. Empathy means that we feel *with* another person rather than *for* that person. It means listening, without ridicule or judgment, as a child expresses her feelings. For example, suppose a child says, "I get scared when you turn out the lights in my room." Instead of our saying, "You big baby, there's nothing to be afraid of," we can simply reflect the child's feeling and encourage the child to talk about it. "You seem a little afraid of the dark. Let's talk about that. Why do you think you are afraid?" In accepting the feeling, the parent accepts the child, thereby revealing unconditional love.

Empathy exists when one person enters the world of another with understanding and compassion. Empathy allows a parent to view a situation through the eyes of the child. A child receives tremendous affirmation when a nonjudgmental parent validates rather than discounts his feelings.

Dr. William Muehl of the Yale Divinity School describes an incident that occurred one December afternoon as parents came to a nursery school to pick up their children. As the children ran toward their parents, each of them carried in his hands a Christmas present on which he had been working for weeks. One little boy, trying to run and put on his coat at the same time, tripped and fell—his colorfully wrapped treasure smashed to pieces on the tile floor in front of him. He sat there and began to cry uncontrollably. His father, hoping to comfort him, stooped down and said, "Don't cry, son. It doesn't matter. It really doesn't matter. Don't cry." But his mother swept the father aside, picked the boy up in her arms, and said, "Oh, but it does matter. It matters a great deal," and she began to weep with her son. Then after the sobbing had abated, she knelt down, helped him pick up the pieces, and said, "Now, let's see what we can make out of what is left."

The mother extended to her son the gift of empathy, and, in so doing, she confirmed the validity of his feelings and his being. It is a priceless form of unconditional love.

In addition to saying "I love you," giving a hug or a pat on the back, eye contact, individual attention, and empathy are ways we can show unconditional love to our child. Giving unconditional love is not just a one-time event; it is a process that requires the constant, on-going attention of the giver. The payoff, however, is tremendous, for we can become the hands and feet of the Christ through whom our children come to accept themselves as persons of great value.

[1]   Matthew 19:15

[2]   "Rewiring the Brain: Early Deprivation and Child Development," *American RadioWorks*,
http://americanradioworks.publicradio.org/features/romania/b1.html

[3]   Robert W. Block, MD, Nancy F. Crebs, MD, and the Committee on Child Abuse and Neglect, and the Committee on Nutrition, The American Academy of Pediatrics, "Failure to Thrive as a Manifestation of Child Neglect," *Pediatrics*, November 1, 2005, pp. 1234–1237.

[4]   Ross Campbell, *How to Really Love Your Child*. Victor Books, 1980, p. 32.

[5]   *Wikipedia*, National Center for Health Statistics, April 2009.

[6]   Matthew 20:30–34.

Discussion Ideas

- How did your parents show you unconditional love? What else might they have done?

- How do you show your child unconditional love? What else can you do?

- This chapter explains several ways of conveying unconditional love. Which makes you feel most loved? Why?

- When Peter and John shared the Gospel with a man begging in front of the temple, they looked intently at him and said, "Look at us" (Acts 3:3–4). Why do you think they wanted to establish eye contact with him? How does it make you feel when you are talking to someone who will not establish eye contact with you?

Chapter 5

Respect (Instead of Fear)

And so we know and rely on the love God has for us. God is love. Whoever lives in love, lives in God, and God in him.... There is no fear in love. But perfect love drives out fear, because fear has to do with punishment. The one who fears is not made perfect in love (1 John 4:16, 18).

A large number of older adults feel that "the primary thing wrong with young people today is that they are not disciplined enough." That generation of parents believed in the philosophy of "spare the rod and spoil the child," and their child-rearing practices worked quite well in terms of producing obedient, authority-fearing children. It is revealing to see, however, the type of relationships such parents have with their children when those children mature into adults themselves.

Many of their grown children say, "When I was little, my father would spank me if I forgot to say, 'Yes, sir,' or, 'No, sir,' to him. I became a very polite child. But I was scared to death of Dad, and I resented him for it." Men in particular tell how they lived in fear of their fathers and that one of the biggest regrets of their lives was the anger that existed between them and their fathers. These men often say, "My dad whipped the dickens out of me when I was a boy, and I turned out okay, didn't I?" But they are stopped in their tracks when asked, "How old were you when you finally came back into relationship with your father?" For most of them, it was not until they were in their thirties or forties, if at all. Many of these grown children, now parents themselves, have decided that life is too short to spend a major part of it in a state of emotional separation from their own children, and they question the use of fear in demanding good behavior from their kids.

Fear-based parenting techniques can produce desired behavior (at least in the short term), but it destroys any possibility of having close relationships with our children. Beatings and other forms of physical and psychological punishment only serve to create bitter children who are scared into "being good" but who basically are not changed inside. Authority-driven parents might argue that the goal is to produce "correct behavior," but truly knowledgeable parents recognize that a more meaningful parenting goal is to produce children who are loving and kind and who are raised to become self-motivated in exercising honesty and integrity.

While a primary objective of ultra-strict, authoritarian parents is to "make our kids respect us," the main response they generate is not one of respect. Parents cannot compel a child's respect. Our children *give* respect to people they admire and whose behavior they would like to copy.

There is a major difference between respect and fear. When we make our children fear us, they feel angry and mistreated. Fear separates people; respect brings people together. Fear produces feelings of resentment and anger; respect is an element of unconditional love.

While fear may be a great tool for producing immediate change, the change it causes is usually superficial and of short duration. Love, on the other hand, generally requires a great deal of time and patience to work its wonders in a person's life; but the change it produces can be lasting and profound. Some of Jesus' followers expected Him to establish His kingdom through means of fear and the sword. Instead, He "parented" them with respect and God's unconditional love—and it worked! That small band of disciples became changed men, and they went about changing the world, witnessing to the power of that love.

The tactics of fear-based parenting include much more than striking or shaking a child. Hurtful words, name-calling, and other spiteful actions can be just as damaging (if not more so) to a child's psyche as is physical abuse. The primary weapon in fear-based parenting is making a child believe that she will have the full love and approval of her parent only if she behaves or performs in a certain way.

A common practice in fear-based parenting is the compensatory attempt to demonstrate love by giving children a lot of "things." The result is a current generation of children who have been given a great deal of material evidence of their parent's affection but who are still unsure as to the sincerity of their parent's love. Parents need to recognize that—whenever it is possible to exercise a choice between spending more time at work to provide more things for their children or spending that same amount of time actually *being* with their kids—placing "time over trinkets" ("presence" over "presents") is a far better expression of unconditional love.

Many parents today are making the conscious choice to move from fear-based to love-based parenting. While still influenced by fear-based techniques that they may have experienced at the hands of *their* parents, they have an inner feeling that there must be a better way. This new style requires that we examine the parenting behaviors of our own parents—keeping those elements that revealed unconditional love and getting rid of those behaviors that were harsh and conditional—and then creating a new parenting model that establishes boundaries and consequences for our children and at the same time shows respect and love.

Love-based parenting means honoring and respecting our child as a child of God. It means loving a child for who she *is* rather than for what she *does*. It requires time, commitment, and the giving of our "selves" to our children by being present in their lives in loving, caring ways. However, parents who understand the concept, and who are willing to work at loving and respecting their children, obtain incredible results.

The Apostle John says that there is no fear in love.[1] The good news for a child whose parents are intentional about giving unconditional love is that she will never have to fear its being withdrawn as a result of her mistakes or misbehavior. One of the reasons why love-based parenting is so effective is because it removes this element of fear. A child blooms when she is blessed by a love she can trust to always be there for her. There is a beautiful story that illustrates the power of love-based parenting.

Walter Wangerin is a Lutheran pastor. His father was the president of Concordia College in Edmonton, Alberta, Canada. When he was a teenager, Walter and his buddies would play football in the hockey rink on the college campus. They played in the springtime when the hockey rink was just earth and grass, and they played in their stocking feet. They always found that over the winter, stones would appear on the field, which had been in the frozen ice. And when they would step on a stone while playing football, they would simply pick it up and throw it off the field until their hockey-rink-football-field would finally be cleared of stones.

Walter had a habit of picking up stones and throwing them at the lights that ringed the hockey rink—enormous 6,000-watt clear globes. Walter figured it was okay to do so because he was a terrible shot and always missed. One day, he picked up a stone and chunked it at the lights. A man from outside of the rink said, "Don't do that!" Walter looked over, and it was his father, the president of the college.

Walter said, "Why not?"

And his dad said, "You'll break a light."

Walter said, "No, no, that's okay. I always miss."

His dad said again, "Don't do that!"

A few days later, Walter stepped on a stone and picked it up and threw it at a light. Here is how Walter describes what followed:

> The instant that that stone left my finger, I knew it was a perfect shot. In slow motion, I saw that stone rise up. Even, clear trajectory. I saw it come right underneath a 6,000-watt clear globe of light. It was like it waited there, looked down at me, winked, and smiled at me. And then it just touched that light. And the most beautiful shower of stone and all of the glass of a 6,000-watt bulb came down in front of me....
>
> Then began for me a hell. I said to Randy, "Don't tell Dad." I said to my brother Paul, "Don't you ever tell Dad about this." I told every kid in the hockey rink, "Don't tell Dad." And then I thought I was safe. Except that when Dad came home for supper that night, I couldn't look at him, because he didn't know what a

terrible son he had, and I felt so guilty underneath his gaze, with his winged eyebrows looking at me....

And so it went for days. Finally, Walter's shame overcame his fear, and he went to talk to his dad.

Presidents of colleges have huge offices. They have enormous oaken doors in front of their offices, and I went to that office. I knocked on my father's door at about the level of a butterfly's kick. And, in the back of my mind, all sorts of voices were talking very, very loud saying, "We're gonna get a spanking. We're gonna get a spanking."

My father said, "Come in." I opened up the door, and there he sat on the other side of the desk, looking at me with his hawk-wing eyebrows and his eyeglasses. He said, "What do you want?"

And I walked to the desk, and I said, "Dad, you know the 6,000-watt light bulb that you said, 'don't hit'?"

He said, "Yes."

I said, "I hit it." And I dropped my eyes because he was looking at me.

For a little while he sat, and then he stood. My father, the president of the college, stood, and he walked around the desk and he came to my side, and I lowered my eyes. And I wished he would have spanked me or punished me, but he didn't do anything. My father, the president of the college, kneeled down beside me and did what I could hardly stand: he killed me with a gesture. My father, the president, put his arms around me and hugged me and loved me. I think he loved me to death. I think his love was more than, for a little while, this child of the night could stand. His love was so good and so bright that I became dust, and then I became raised up.

Because, don't you know, that when we go through those changes of becoming dust, the love doesn't cease….All along it was the thing that we did not deserve. My father hugged me, and I did what I wouldn't have done if he had spanked me—I cried, and I changed, and I came to the light. It always was love. It never was condemnation…in my father, it always was love. And I became in that moment, not just before my father, don't you understand, because it was Jesus who was in my father—Jesus who saw steadily into the depths of my soul—I became in such a hug, in such a steadiness of watching, in such a brightness of light, I became a child of my father, and of the light, and of God. To that I didn't say then, but I do say now, Amen.[2]

When we embrace our children with respect and forgiveness as Walter Wangerin's father received him that day, we receive our children as Jesus did. Walter's father did not bust him for poor performance; he just loved and accepted his boy without condition. Fear may change behavior, but it does not change the child. Only love and respect can do that. And so it is with love-based parenting.

In J. D. Salinger's book, *The Catcher in the Rye*, Holden Caulfield says, "I keep seeing all these little children, tumbling down some hill of rye and all...and there is no one around to catch them. I mean as they stray or as they start to go over the cliff. Somebody must be there to catch them. That's what I must do...I must become the Catcher in the Rye!!"[3]

Like Walter Wangerin's father and Holden Caulfield, may we catch our children and lift them up and enable them to value themselves as lovable, forgivable children of God. It is called love-based parenting. I ask you: is there a more powerful and wonderful way to serve as the hands and feet of the Christ?

---

[1] 1 John 4:18.
[2] Walter Wangerin Jr., "Into the World, Not to Condemn the World," *30GoodMinutes*, Program 3021, First air date March 1, 1987.
[3] J. D. Salinger, *The Catcher in the Rye*, 1951.

Discussion Ideas

- What type of parenting model were you raised with—love-based or fear-based? Were the parenting models employed by your mother and your father basically the same or profoundly different?

- The Old Testament often features an angry God who punishes those who disobey His will. Jesus reveals a God Who unconditionally forgives and loves. How do you view God?

- Did you ever experience feelings of anger or resentment toward your parents as a result of being the recipient of fear-based parenting? If so, have you reconciled with your parents? Have those feelings been resolved?

- How do you hope your child would describe you as a parent?

Chapter 6

Encouragement (Instead of Praise)

Therefore encourage one another and build each other up, just as in fact you are doing (1 Thessalonians 5:11).

S table, positive family environments do not just happen. They are created through planning and hard work. A primary factor in building positive relationships is the constant, intentional use of encouragement. Adults need the encouragement of one another to live confident, productive, joyful lives. Encouragement is essential to the psychological and spiritual growth of our children as well. In his seminal book *Children: the Challenge*, Dr. Rudolf Dreikurs says:

> Encouragement is more important than any other aspect of child raising. It is so important that the lack of it can be considered the basic cause of misbehavior. *A misbehaving child is a discouraged child....* When a child makes a mistake or fails to accomplish a certain goal, we must avoid any word or

action which indicates that we consider *him* a failure....*we need to separate the deed from the doer.* We must have it clear in our own minds that each "failure" indicates only a lack of skill and in no way affects the *value* of the person. Courage is found in one who can make a mistake and fail without feeling lowered in his self-esteem. This "courage to be imperfect" is equally needed by children and adults. Without it, discouragement is inevitable.[1]

Because it "separates the deed from the doer" and affirms a person's worth in spite of her mistakes, encouragement is a key element in the giving of unconditional love and a sense of high self-esteem.

Encouragement also helps build a person's sense of self-worth. All human beings have a need to find their place in this world—to discover a sense of self-respect and accomplishment—through work and achievement. As Craig Reynolds alluded, encouragement helps remove the "performance-pressure" and gives people the courage to take some risks and to try their best without the fear of failure. Encouragement, therefore, builds both self-worth and self-esteem—the two components of a person's self-concept.

In promoting a child's self-concept, a word needs to be said about the difference between "praise" and "encouragement." Praise focuses on a child's performance and achievements, while encouragement focuses on a child's efforts to achieve. That concept is so important that I am going to say it again in a slightly different way. Praise compliments the *results,* while encouragement compliments the *effort.*

Encouragement bolsters a child's self-confidence and enables her to proceed with courage and a sense of purpose in spite of her mistakes. Praise, on the other hand, can be a source of discouragement, because a child can be led to believe that she is of value only if she achieves and performs well.

If our child tells us that his team won the city's peewee baseball championship, a word of *praise* might be, "That's great, Robby. You're a real champ!" An *encouraging* statement might be, "I know you've worked very hard practicing baseball, Robby. You can really be proud of yourself." Praise allows a child to feel good about himself when he is successful. Encouragement allows a child to feel good about himself constantly—even when he does not achieve first place.

A girls' high school soccer team was playing in the finals for the state championship. They won by a score of 2-0. The goalkeeper had a brilliant game. When she came off the field, her father told her, "As I watched you out there, I was reminded of all the hard work you've exerted in practice that enabled you to play like you did today. I am so proud of you!" The next season, her team played in the state finals again. This time, their defense broke down, and the goalkeeper was like a target in a shooting gallery. They were beaten by a score of 6-1. When the goalkeeper came off the field that day, her father said, "You never gave up. Through all the blood, sweat, and tears, you kept fighting. I'm so proud of you!"

In both instances, her encouraging father complimented the goalkeeper's efforts rather than the end result, and the girl felt good about her participation in both games. That is the power of encouragement. As opposed to praise, it allows a child of any age to feel valued regardless of the outcome of the game in which she is participating.

There are two things that parents commonly do, hoping to encourage their child, but that actually serve to discourage him.

One source of discouragement can be parental overprotection. Sometimes parents are overzealous in protecting their children from even minor experiences of pain or failure. When we do so, we diminish a child's sense of self-competency, which, in turn, leads to feelings of discouragement. While we should be present to observe, a five-year-old child can safely navigate the equipment at the average playground without the interference of an adult. Occasional scratches and misadventures can be great learning tools. Making mistakes and incurring a little bit of pain also help a child to understand that life is an adventure and that she can be an excellent person without being perfect.

A second cause of discouragement can be the comparisons that parents make. Making comparisons among children does not serve as an encouragement to them. This is especially true of children who are brothers and sisters. The lower-achieving child is only further reminded of the hopelessness of his situation, and the higher-achieving child often begins to feel anxious about trying to stay ahead. Every child is a child of God and wonderfully different and unique. Encouraging parents intentionally focus on the individual child without subjecting him to comparisons with others.

The task of encouraging children often requires a great deal of creativity and persistence. A teacher invited Dr. Dreikurs to observe her classroom one afternoon. In front of the class, the teacher complained about a particular student's poor handwriting skills. She explained that the class had been practicing writing the letter "O" and showed Dreikurs the student's sheet of paper. It was an absolute mess, with scribbling all over the page. Dreikurs took the paper and studied it for several minutes. Finally, he smiled at the teacher and the student, pointed to the only legible letter on the page, and said, "That's a pretty nicely shaped 'O' right there." The student took the paper and returned to his desk. A few minutes later, he showed Dreikurs and the teacher an entire page of beautifully shaped "O's."[2] An adult encourager can play an incredibly positive role in the life of a child.

In his book *The Seven Habits of Highly Effective People*, Stephen Covey suggests that family members establish an "Emotional

Bank Account" with each other.[3] Through words of encouragement, we make deposits into the Emotional Bank Account of our children, and the result is a high trust level and good communication. With a surplus of "goodwill deposits" in the account, parents and children are able to engage in their occasional confrontations and still continue to honor and respect each other.

We make withdrawals from the Emotional Bank Account through disrespect, criticism, and threats. All too often, the discouraging remarks directed at our children far outnumber the words of encouragement, and the Emotional Bank Account gets overdrawn. The result is alienation and distrust. People become bitter and defensive, and both sides have to walk around on eggshells in hopes of not offending each other.

As He walked among people, Jesus was a tremendous encourager to those around Him. Priests, disciples, prostitutes, tax collectors, poor people, rich people, and thieves all received His words of encouragement. Even when He was dying on a cross, Jesus turned to one of the thieves who was crucified alongside Him and said, "Truly, I tell you, today you will be with me in Paradise."[4] Keenly aware of the power of encouragement in instilling resilience and hope, Jesus would lovingly and persistently encourage His child.

To create warm, caring relationships with children, parents can ask themselves on a daily basis, "Have my deposits into my children's account exceeded my withdrawals today?" Building a child's positive self-concept through encouragement is a central task of a loving parent.

[1] Rudolf Dreikurs, *Children: The Challenge.* Penguin Books, 1987, pp. 36, 38.
[2] Bill and Kathy Kvols-Riedler, *Redirecting Children's Misbehavior.* R.D.I.C. Publications, 1979, p. 137.
[3] Stephen Covey, *The 7 Habits of Highly Effective People.* Simon and Schuster, 1989, p. 188.
[4] Luke 23:43.

Discussion Ideas

- Give some examples of the difference between encouragement and praise.

- Have you ever compared a lower-achieving child to a higher-achieving child? How do you think each child felt?

- Describe a time when a child's failure to live up to his parent's expectations visibly upset his parent. Do you think the pressure or anger exhibited was helpful to the child?

- What would you estimate to be the ratio of deposits to withdrawals that you make into your child's Emotional Bank Account each week? What are some ways in which you could make more weekly deposits into your child's account?

Chapter 7
Learning (Instead of Ignorance)

I did not listen to the voice of my teachers or incline my ear to my instructors. Now I am at the point of utter ruin in the public assembly (Proverbs 5:13-14).

The Importance of Learning

As I mentioned earlier, I was raised in a west Texas town called Odessa. The late Molly Ivins wrote a column for *The Texas Observer* in which she described the town's bid for a four-year college. Molly said:

> The Texas State College Coordinating Board put out a notice that a new four-year college was going to be created somewhere in west Texas. Odessa and its nearby football rival, Midland, erupted with college fever—with the two town newspapers blasting each other, and the local citizenry aroused as if a district football championship was at stake.

The powers in Midland hired a fancy lawyer from former Texas Governor John Connally's law firm in Houston to represent them before the Coordinating Board. Odessa, on the other hand, hired one of its own, a local talent named Warren Burnett.

The City Fathers of Odessa had long suspected Warren Burnett of being a card-carrying communist on account of he sometimes defended poor people for free. But they knew he was the best lawyer in the state, and so they gritted their teeth and hired him to represent their case.

Which he did, magniloquently, grandiloquently, for more than two hours without interruption. I was privileged to hear it. At the end of Burnet's speech, the chairman of the Coordinating Board said, "Mr. Burnett, this has indeed been a most impressive presentation. I am left with just one question to ask you. Do you honestly believe there is justification for a four-year college in Odessa?"

Burnett beamed and replied, "Mr. Chairman, there is enough ignorance in Odessa to justify an eight-year college." Got the school too.[1]

The dictionary definition of "ignorance" is "lack of education," and, while Warren Burnett was speaking tongue-in-cheek, he also spoke the truth. Early Odessa was an "oil patch" town with a sizable percentage of the population consisting of "roughnecks" who fed the pipe into the big rigs. There *was* a lot of ignorance in Odessa, and the town did need the school.

The danger inherent in ignorance is that when we know little of the world or of the people who populate it, it can be a breeding ground for prejudice, discrimination, and indifference. How do we dispel ignorance? What is needed is an environment—at home and at school—that encourages learning.

Great learning can take place most anywhere. People can learn how to relate to others, how to perform a job well, and how to seek life's deeper meanings in a variety of venues. Oil field workers and brain surgeons alike can be avid learners. It involves keeping one's mind open to new perspectives and fresh ideas. And it almost always is the product of encouragement.

A central task of adults in delivering our society's children from the tyranny of ignorance is to encourage learning.

What Schools Can Do...

Kids today need at least a high school education. Without that basic learning experience, children will be totally unprepared to successfully function within society's increasingly complex socioeconomic structures and to participate in a meaningful way in the world's future economy. Unfortunately, American education today is in a crisis mode. Over thirty percent of all students drop out of high school without a diploma.[2] And, in many of our major inner-city school districts, the dropout rate is over fifty percent.

After doing a lot of soul-searching, educational leaders are beginning to understand that a key element in encouraging kids to obtain an education is a positive learning environment. *How* we teach is as important as *what* we teach.

One such learning environment was my Algebra II class at Odessa High School. It was taught by Milton Kuser, a man with five college degrees (including two law degrees) who chose to spend his life teaching kids. While sometimes gruff-acting and always demanding, he was a great encourager. He joked and cajoled and made his students feel like he truly cared about them and their education. His expectations and his demands for excellence helped inspire in those kids a positive attitude regarding the importance of learning.

Of the thirty-one students in Mr. Kuser's class, twenty-five went on to obtain postgraduate college degrees. Many came from very modest home situations. For example, John Belcher, whose father was an oil field roughneck and only finished the seventh grade, became the division head for Astrophysics at MIT. While other factors were at work in those students' lives, Milton Kuser surely played a role in helping inspire a desire to learn. He created a positive learning environment—the signature trademark of great teachers and great schools.

Dr. Ralph Draper, former superintendent of the Spring ISD (Houston, Texas) told his teachers, "There are two things you can control in the classroom: the nature of the relationship and the nature of the work. The relationship comes first. If the relationship between teacher and student is not in place, the kids aren't going to produce the work. The key to the process is to develop a relationship that is love-based instead of fear-based, and kids can sense the difference."[3]

What Parents Can Do

Even more important than the school in encouraging learning is the role played by the parent.

Many parents think that a child's success at school is the responsibility of the teacher. Teachers *are* important in helping children to receive a first-rate education. However, research indicates that parents have a much greater effect than teachers in regard to younger children's success at school.

When Jesus was twelve, He spent three days in the great temple in Jerusalem listening to the teachers and asking them questions, and "all who heard Him were amazed at His understanding and His answers."[4] How did this young boy manage to hold His own with those great scholars? One reason had to be because He had been encouraged and supported by His parents in his early schooling at the synagogue.

Few children excel at school without the high expectations, involvement, and encouragement of their parents. In fact, several studies have found that the "home effect" is far greater than the "school effect" and accounts for approximately sixty percent of the average student achievement.[56] So, parents, be put on notice:

If you want your child to be successful at school, you must get involved in—and encourage—your child's academic activities!

The Early Childhood Years

Parent involvement in the early years from birth to age four is especially critical.

Drs. Betty Hart and Todd Risley worked with parents and children from a variety of income levels to determine how preschool experiences in the home impacted children's academic careers. They recorded the interactions of parents and their children. The study focused on the number of words heard by children during the first four years of their lives, a time when learning vocabulary skills and brain development are heavily linked.

Hart and Risley's research made a very, very important discovery. They found that, although young children from low-income families tend to grade lower on intelligence tests than children from more affluent families, it is *no*t because low-income children are less intelligent. They simply are at a disadvantage in terms of the size of their vocabulary.

Their research found that children in poverty families heard an average of 616 words per hour. In working-class families, children heard an average of 1,251 words per hour, while children in professional families heard 2,153 words per hour. Hart and Risley reported, "In four years of such experience, an average child in a professional family would have accumulated experience with almost 45 million words...and an average child in a welfare family would have accumulated experience with 13 million words."[7] This 32 million "word advantage" explains why four-year-old children raised in higher-income families tend to score much higher on intelligence tests than children who are raised in a culture of generational poverty.

In identifying the huge disparity in vocabulary skills among children from different socioeconomic classes, Hart and Risley are not pointing fingers of blame. Their study simply identified important cultural differences that can result in potentially smart low-income children not developing the skills that would lead them to score well on intelligence tests. The good news is that when low-income parents are armed with the knowledge that vocabulary skills are an important part of early childhood brain development, they can begin interacting with their children in ways that will close the "word gap."

In his book *Children: Behavior and Development*, Dr. Boyd McCandless says, "Language development during infancy has been shown to be more highly related to later tests of intelligence than any other measure of infant 'intelligence.'" He then adds these words of hope: "With adult attention, the language development of infants can be accelerated: for example, the more reading infants have been exposed to, the more advanced their language development is likely to be...regardless of the social class from which they come."[8]

Parents, it is vitally important that you read to your small children! And it helps to have magazines and lots of children's books visible around the house. When children see written materials in the home, it conveys the message that words and books are important. Also, spending time sitting with your child, reading to him, listening to music, singing with him, and visiting the library together are wonderful ways of conveying unconditional love.

If you want to help your child be successful at school, spend time with your small child...talk with her and read to her. You can make a tremendous difference—just as Jesus' parents did with Him.

Kindergarten through High School

Here are some things that parents can do to promote success in school for their children:

- Make sure your child knows that you think education is important and that you expect her to be successful at school. Your high expectations of your child will encourage her to have high expectations of herself.

- Insist that your child stay in school and do his very best. Be sure he understands that a high school graduate makes an average of $26,933 per year, while someone without a high school degree will average making only $17,299 per year— a difference of almost $10,000 per year! [9] If your child does not get a diploma, he most likely will spend his life doing menial jobs, existing on welfare, and living out the words of Proverbs: "I did not listen to the voice of my teachers or incline my ear to my instructors. Now I am at the point of utter ruin in the public assembly." [10]

- Have some magazines and books around the house—items that signal your interest in reading and that encourage your child to read.

- Insist that your child do her homework. Set up a time and a place for your child to do that homework. Encourage your child to be responsible and to work independently.

- Show up! Attend your child's activities at the school to show support for him. Your gift of time is a way of demonstrating unconditional love.

- Participate in parent activities at your child's school. Volunteer in a classroom, in the library, tutoring, or reading to a class. Attend PTA/PTO or parent-booster club meetings. That involvement lets your child know that you think her education is important.

- If there is any area of concern, stay in touch with your child's teacher. Ask for a parent/teacher conference. Envision you and the teacher working together as a team to promote your child's success at school.

The role that parents can play in helping their child to be successful at school is enormous. Your child's performance is a self-worth issue. However, the time you spend reading to your child, supervising homework, showing up for school activities, and giving encouragement is a gift of unconditional love and also elevates your child's self-esteem.

To enhance His child's success at school, Jesus would get involved. We should do the same.

[1]   Molly Ivins, "A Creature of the Courts: Warren Burnett," *Texas Observer*, October 10, 2002, http://www.texasobserver.org/article.php?aid=1132

[2]   The Alliance for Excellent Education, 2006.

[3]   A conversation with Dr. Ralph Draper, Houston, Texas, April 5, 2012.

[4]   Luke 2:46–47.

[5]   B. Hart, and T. R. Risley, Meaningful Differences in the Everyday Experiences of Young American Children, Paul H. Brookes Publishing, 1995.

6   C. Lubienski and S. T. Lubienski, *Charter, Private and Public Schools and Academic Achievement: New evidence from NAEP mathematics data.* New York: National Center for the Study of Privatization in Education, 2006.

7   "Reducing disparities through vocabulary skills," *Dallas Morning News,* November 17, 2011.

8   Boyd R. McCandless, *Children: Behavior and Development,* 1967, p. 373.

9   U.S. Bureau of the Census, 2006.

10 Proverbs 5:13–14.

Discussion Ideas

- In what ways can you become more involved in parent activities at your child's school?

- When are the best times for regularly scheduled reading times—or supervised study—with your children?

- Mary had high expectations of Jesus regarding his intellectual progress (Luke 2:45–52). What are your expectations for your child's success at school? How do you share those expectations with your child?

- How could you team up with your child's teacher to promote your child's success at school?

PART III

Jesus' Response to a Child's Misbehavior

Chapter 8

When You Are Trying to Figure Out What Is Wrong...

Even a child is known by his actions, by whether his conduct is pure and right (Proverbs 20:11).

D r. Rudolf Dreikurs emphasizes that the worldwide movement toward democracy can be seen not only among nations but also in our families and schools. Our children believe that they have a right to participate in the democratic process—which helps explain the questioning of authority now commonplace in our homes and classrooms. Dreikurs believes that the old autocratic parenting model, with its emphasis upon control and authority, is not workable in a world that is pushing toward democracy. He calls for democratic child-rearing practices based on principles of equality and mutual respect.

In a family democracy, parents are "first among equals." Their role as co-presidents is based upon their knowledge, competency, experience, and the responsibilities entrusted to them. However, while ultimate authority in the family rests with the parents, children have "equality" with the adults in terms of dignity and human worth. Everyone within the democracy is equally entitled to respect.

In relating to their children through a respectful democratic model, it is important that parents have some insight into the reasons for children's misbehavior. All children want to behave. They want the approval of their parents and their peers. Misbehavior takes place only when children do not have their needs met.

Jesus had a genius for recognizing people's unmet needs. Often, they came to Him complaining about emotional or physical pain they were experiencing, and He would address the deeper, spiritual needs causing the pain. People hunched over their desks making a god out of their work sometimes develop neck and back pains because of muscle constriction. Folks in stressful, argumentative relationships often experience stomach aches and ulcers caused by the secretion of excessive stomach acid. Most alcohol and drug addiction is caused by unmet emotional needs.

Part of the reason why Jesus had such great healing success is because He had such great intuitive understanding of how stress impacts psychosomatic illness. Inappropriate activation of the involuntary nervous system and the internal secretion glands can cause real structural damage to the body.[1] In fact, all illness has some psychosomatic factors, because the body reflects our mental, emotional, and spiritual health. Shame and guilt, in particular, wreak great damage upon the human psyche.

Over and over again, Jesus told the people, "Your sins are forgiven. Now take up your bed and walk." He recognized the underlying spiritual needs that give rise to much of people's pain and misbehavior. Then, as He healed them spiritually, they were also released from their emotional and physical pain.

Jesus would have great appreciation of child-rearing practices that deal with misbehavior by first asking the question, "What is my child's unmet need?"

Understanding Why Children Misbehave

There are three basic human needs: *the need to be loved and wanted*; *the need to feel powerful*; and *the need for life to be meaningful and fun*.[2] Dr. Dreikurs says that misbehavior occurs when children try to fill their unmet needs in inappropriate ways. He says that every bad behavior can be connected to a specific unmet need.[3]

Connecting misbehaviors with unmet needs:

For example, some common misbehaviors—and the corresponding unmet needs they seek to fill—are as follows:

- When a child seeks <u>attention</u> in improper ways, he is trying to fill the <u>need to be loved and wanted</u>.

- If a child starts initiating <u>power struggles</u>, he is attempting to address the <u>need to be more powerful</u> and to have some control over his life.

- If a child is <u>rebellious</u>, she typically is bored and is pursuing her <u>need to make life more meaningful and fun</u>.

Children do not consciously seek to misbehave; they unconsciously resort to a particular misbehavior in hopes of meeting an unmet need. Parents often take it personally when their children misbehave. They ask, "Why is my child attacking me like this?" Instead of feeling defensive when confronted by a child's misbehavior, the important question for an adult to ask is, "What is the unmet need of this child?"

If a parent can identify the child's unmet need and then proceed to fill that need, the child's disruptive behavior will disappear. The key to this process lies in accurately connecting the particular misbehavior with its corresponding unmet need and then responding to that need in a helpful way.

Connecting feelings with misbehaviors and their corresponding unmet needs:

Some child-rearing experts say that if an adult examines his own feelings when confronted by a child's misbehavior, he usually can connect the child's misbehavior with the related unmet need.[4] For example,

If a parent feels <u>annoyed</u> by a child's misbehavior, the child is seeking negative attention; and the corresponding unmet need is to feel loved and wanted.

If a parent feels <u>angry</u> as a result of a child's actions, the child is seeking power through confrontation; and the corresponding unmet need is for a greater sense of power and control over his life.

If an adult feels <u>guilty</u> in regard to her competency as a parent, the child is acting rebellious; and the corresponding unmet need is for life to be more meaningful and fun.

(See the "The Misbehavior Chart" on page 128.)

With patience and practice, a parent can become adept at identifying a child's unmet need by a quick self-evaluation of how the child's misbehavior makes the parent feel. The parent can then address the disruptive behavior by nurturing an attention-seeking child; empowering a power-seeking child; and making home life more interesting and entertaining for a rebellious child. Identifying the underlying unmet need is a key element in understanding, and dealing with, a misbehaving child.

Mary was working on her bank statement. It was not something she enjoyed. She was not fond of numbers and math; but, to keep the family's financial records straight, it was something she made a point of doing every Saturday morning.

Mary's eight-year-old daughter, Tamara, came into the room and walked over to the desk where Mary was working. Tamara grabbed hold of her mother's upper left arm and gave it a shake. "Hey, Mom, I built this incredible castle with Legos in my room. Come give it a look!"

Mary said, "Not now, Tamara, I'm busy."

Tamara, smiled and shook her arm harder. "Oh, c'mon, Mom, it'll just take a second."

Mary shook her head, said "No," and kept on working. Tamara leaned over and put her face in front of her mother's face, blocking Mary's view of her papers. "It's unbelievable, Mom. Come see it!"

Mary said, "Tamara, I'm working! This is annoying and…."

Mary caught herself in midsentence. What did I just say? That I'm feeling "annoyed"? Thinking quickly, Mary recalled that if a child's behavior in annoying, it is a sign that the behavior is attention-seeking. And a child who is seeking negative attention has a need to feel loved and wanted.

Mary smiled back at Tamara's grinning face and said, "Tamara, give me five minutes to finish totaling these figures, and then I'll come see what you've built. And, while we're at it, why don't you and I build a barn next to the castle so the king and queen will have a place to keep their horses?"

Mary modeled the three basic steps in dealing with a misbehaving child. When a child misbehaves:

- Based on how the child's behavior makes you feel, determine the specific type of misbehavior.

- Connect the misbehavior with the corresponding unmet need.

- Address that unmet need, and the misbehavior will disappear.

Too often, when a child misbehaves, the parent will get upset or take the behavior as a personal affront. "Why is that kid acting so ornery toward me?" Jesus would look beyond the outward behavior and ask the deeper question, "What is the unmet need of my child?" He would proceed to meet that need, and the misbehavior would go away.

[1] "Psychosomatic Disorder." *Encyclopædia Britannica. Encyclopædia Britannica Online.* Encyclopædia Britannica Inc., 2012. Web. 10 Apr. 2012. <http://www.britannica.com/EBchecked/topic/481834/psychosomatic-disorder>.

[2] William Glasser, *The Quality School Teacher.* Harper Perennial, 1993, p. 137.

[3] Rudolf Dreikurs, *Children: The Challenge.* Penguin Books, 1964, pp. 58–64.

[4] Don Dinkmeyer and Gary D. McKay, *The Parent's Handbook.* Circle Pines, Minnesota: American Guidance Service, 1989, p. 9.

Discussion Ideas

- Share an illustration of an attention-seeking child, a rebellious child, and a power-seeking child.

- Can you think of an instance when you would have handled the situation differently had you considered the unmet need of your child?

- Describe a time when your own unmet need resulted in your behaving inappropriately. How could you have responded differently?

- In the majority of cases when your child misbehaves, is there a particular feeling that misbehavior evokes in you? Based on how that behavior makes you feel, what would you guess is your child's most prevalent unmet need?

Chapter 9

When You Are Feeling Really Annoyed…
(Dealing with an Attention-Seeking Child)

Leah became pregnant and gave birth to a son. She named him Reuben, for she said, "It is because the LORD has seen my misery. Surely my husband will love me now." She conceived again, and when she gave birth to a son she said, "Because the LORD heard that I am not loved, he gave me this one too."…Again she conceived, and when she gave birth to a son she said, "Now at last my husband will become attached to me, because I have borne him three sons" (Genesis 29:32–34).

Of the three basic human needs, the most important is *to feel loved and wanted.* If a child believes that the only way she can feel loved and can experience a sense of belonging is through demanding attention, she will prefer negative attention to no attention at all. In a *Newsweek* article, one young killer was quoted as saying, "I had rather be wanted for murder than not wanted at all."[1]

How do you know if you are dealing with an attention-seeking child? The "tip-off" for a parent who is trying to identify the unmet need in a misbehaving child is to examine the feelings that the parent is experiencing as a result of the child's actions. If the feelings are ones of annoyance or frustration, then the child's unmet need is to feel loved and wanted. And the means of filling this need will be an inappropriate attempt to call attention to herself.

Young and old, people who feel unloved will resort to all kinds of unhealthy behaviors in hopes of getting others to love them. Like poor Leah, whose plight is depicted in the pages of the Old Testament, many girls who feel unloved or unwanted at home will try to win love by having sex and babies. As a former gang leader of the Crips in Los Angeles explained, "If you don't receive unconditional love and acceptance at home, you'll try to find it on the streets."[2]

The most common form of misbehavior at home and at school is perpetrated by the attention-seeking child seeking reassurance that she is loved and wanted.

Did you ever wonder what Jesus' "elevator message" would be if He only had three seconds between floors to share His main message with someone? Really, it is a no-brainer. He would say, "You are unconditionally loved by God." If we were the other person on that elevator, we might think, What was that about? But the truth is: if we do not feel unconditionally loved and valued as a child of God, we probably are going to spend our lives trying to draw attention to ourselves in inappropriate, superficial, and unfulfilling ways. Therefore, it is vital that parents strive to become vessels through whom God's unconditional love is poured into the lives of their children.

In dealing with an attention-seeking child, the most important task of the parent is to extend the unconditional acceptance and love that says to the child, "I love you. You belong in this family. As problems arise, we will solve them together." When a child's craving for love and a sense of belonging is satisfied through the nurturing of a caring parent, it helps lessen the need for disruptive, attention-seeking behavior.

One tactic in dealing with an attention-demanding child is to give the child attention when he is not expecting it. The trick is to "catch the child doing something good." Parents should be on the lookout for instances of positive behavior, and, prior to any demand upon the part of the child, "surprise" the child with an expression of appreciation for that behavior. For example, if your child picks up her clothes to take them to the clothes hamper, you might say, "I really appreciate your efforts to keep your room clean."

This tactic of surprising attention-seekers with attention when they are not expecting it is effective with both children and adults. Jesus' disciple Peter was an attention-seeker, always asking questions and drawing attention to himself and bragging about how he would never forsake Jesus in times of danger. One time, when Jesus was talking with His disciples, He asked them who they thought He was. Peter replied, "You are the Messiah, the Son of the Living God." This was the first time any of His disciples grasped who Jesus was. Peter was listening to, and comprehending, Jesus' teachings in a manner that others had not, and Jesus surprised Peter with these affirming words, "You are Peter, and on this rock, I will build my church."[3] That positive, unexpected attention helped meet Peter's unmet need to feel loved and wanted.

Another approach parents can use in helping attention-seeking kids is to not reward a child's attempt to get negative attention. If a kid is able to draw attention to himself through misbehavior, he will be encouraged to continue the tactic. So, if possible, a parent should not pay attention to negative behavior. When it is impractical to ignore an attention-seeking child, parents can use a *self-evaluation technique* as a means of getting the disruptive kid to think about what he is doing and, hopefully, to change his inappropriate behavior.[4] Utilizing a calm, nonjudgmental voice, the parent can ask the child:

"What are you doing?"

"What should you be doing?"

"What are you going to do right now?"

Each parent can develop his or her own questions that are designed to help a child become aware of his disruptive, attention-seeking behavior. It is important that these responses be delivered in a firm, yet caring and nonjudgmental voice. If the parent's voice carries even a hint of annoyance or frustration, the child will feel attacked, and the inappropriate behavior will continue.

Here is how one parent dealt with his attention-seeking child:

James pulled his car into the driveway at his home. He looked at his watch. It was four o'clock in the afternoon. As he walked in the front door, his six-year-old Tonya descended upon him. He smiled. He really had not seen his daughter this entire week. The twelve-hour work days had put him at home each night just as she was going to bed. However, today was Friday, and James had decided to leave the office early.

As Tonya rushed up to him, James reached down and gave her a kiss and then smiled as she wrapped her little body around his leg. She laughed and giggled as he literally dragged her through the hallway and into the kitchen. He kissed his wife hello, and, still dragging Tonya, made his way to the family room and collapsed in his favorite chair. Feeling a little bit annoyed by her clinging, he said, "Let go, Tonya." She just giggled and hugged him even tighter.

James reached down, peeled the little girl off his leg, and picked up the newspaper from the lamp table alongside his chair. He thought, It will be so good to just relax and disengage from what has been a really exhausting week at the office. Tonya, however, moved around to the other side of his chair and started pulling on his shirtsleeve as he tried to read. He said, "Just a minute, sweetheart. Let me read a little bit."

She kept pulling on his sleeve and started whining, "Daddy, Daddy, Daddy, come on, Daddy. I want to show you the new shoes Mother got me today."

Really starting to feel irritated, James said, "Not now, Tonya. I'll look at them later."

"Now, Daddy, now," she insisted, still pulling at his shirtsleeve.

Frustrated by her annoying behavior, James started to say something sharp to Tonya but then caught himself. Looking her in the eye, James said, "Tonya, what are you doing? How about going and getting the shoes and bringing them to me?" Startled, the girl thought about his words for a couple of seconds and let go of his sleeve. As she started out of the room, James said, "Listen, honey, I've got an even better idea. Go put those shoes on. I'll be done with the newspaper in ten minutes, and we'll walk down to the park together." True to his word, James laid down his paper ten minutes later, grabbed Tonya by the hand, and walked with her to the local park.

As he pushed her in a swing, James asked Tonya how her school had been going. He also told her, "Your mother tells me you bathed the dog yesterday. I really admire your hard work, Tonya." Tonya beamed—the whiny behavior all gone.

What took place here? Tonya had not seen her father in a week. So, when she finally got her chance, she started demanding his attention. When somebody you care about is not paying attention to you, then negative attention is better than no attention at all. James's tip-off was the way in which his daughter's misbehavior made him feel. Her whiny, clingy behavior was annoying and frustrating, and he recognized that those are the feelings generated by an attention-seeking child—a child whose unmet need is to feel wanted and loved.

James handled the situation beautifully. He did not reward her attempts to get negative attention. He did not drop what he was doing to go look at her new shoes. Instead, he asked her to stop and think about what she was doing and suggested she choose an alternate behavior. Then, he surprised her with the invitation to go to the park together—thereby giving her attention in ways that she was not expecting. And later, he "caught her doing something good," and complimented her giving the dog a bath. He gave her attention—in positive, affirming ways that made Tonya feel wanted and loved. And, after all, that is what attention-seeking behavior is all about.

A loving, caring home environment is essential in conveying to children that they are valued members of the family. When kids feel confident that they are loved and that they belong, they will no longer need to seek negative attention.

Jesus gave children His attention. Once, when parents were bringing their children to Him to be blessed by Him, His disciples tried to shoo them away, saying that Jesus was too busy to be bothered by them. Jesus quickly intervened. He said, "Let the little children come to me and do not stop them."[5] Jesus made children feel loved and wanted and invites us to do the same with our child.

[1] Sharon Begley, "Why the Young Kill," *Newsweek*, May 2, 1999, pp. 52–56.
[2] Quote from panel member at the "1996 White House Conference on Youth, Drugs, and Violence."
[3] Matthew 16:15–18.
[4] William Glasser, The Quality School: Managing Students without Coercion. Harper Perennial, 1992, p. 272.
[5] Matthew 19:13–14.

Discussion Ideas

- If your child frequently seeks attention in a negative manner, what might be ways of reducing those occurrences in the future?
- Can you think of an instance when you would have handled an attention-seeking incident differently had you considered the unmet need of your child?
- Think of a person whose behavior you find annoying and frustrating. What do you think they need from you? What changes can you make to improve the relationship?
- Jesus' ministry was built on giving people positive attention and helping them to feel loved and wanted by God. In what ways can you be intentional in sharing God's love, especially with your child?

Chapter 10

When You Are Wanting to
Show Who Is Boss...
(Dealing with a Power-Seeking Child)

God blessed them, and God said to them, "Be
fruitful and multiply, and fill the earth and subdue it;
and have dominion over the fish of the sea and over the
birds of the air and over every living thing that moves
upon the earth" (Genesis 1:28).

God created humankind to have power—to have dominion over all the earth. It is in our DNA. It is no wonder then that one of the three primary human needs is the need *to feel powerful.* Children who consistently engage in power struggles are searching for ways to fill that need. Even young children have a need to feel respected and to know they can make some decisions and exercise some control over their destiny.

Jesus said, "The Spirit of the Lord is on me, because He has anointed me to proclaim good news to the poor. He has sent me to proclaim freedom for the prisoners and recovery of sight for the blind, to set the oppressed free."[1] Jesus recognized people's need for some power in their lives, and He tried to empower those around Him who had been beaten down by the world and who felt bereft of any personal power. And, in standing up for those who felt helpless and hopeless, Jesus engaged in some fierce power struggles against the people who were oppressing them.

Psychiatrist William Adler wrote in *The Will to Power* that virtually every human interaction has within it the elements of a power struggle. His observations ring true both in regard to relationships between adults and in relationships between adults and their children.

Parent-child power struggles are natural, normal, and appropriate—especially when children are moving through the developmental stages where they are attempting to declare their personhood. When adults hear ourselves say, "I'll show you who is boss!" we know from our own angry response that the child's goal is power. Children who consistently engage in power struggles are searching for ways to have more control over their lives. As adults, our role is to find safe, responsible ways for our children to feel more powerful.

Parents can help take some of the rough edges off these struggles by communicating to their children that not only do they value and cherish them, but they also respect them. Respect is demonstrated by our asking for their opinions, listening to them, and then showing some genuine concern for their thoughts and feelings. We can say, "Caroline, we seem to have a problem here. I know that, together, you and I can solve it. Tell me what you think." The simple act of listening shows respect to children and gives them a sense of power.

Another means of easing the power struggle is to remove all the unnecessary rules. An essential part of the adult role is to sort out the trivial from that which is truly important. Too often, parents give too much attention to "side issues"—demanding that children eat all their vegetables and keep their rooms "hospital clean"—instead of focusing on three or four rules that are absolutely essential to family peace and harmony (no physical or emotional abuse, no drugs, a reasonable curfew, letting other family members know where you are, etc.).

Parents should also try to avoid creating "win/lose" situations with children. Rather than offering kids "yes or no" solutions, we can offer them choices between two acceptable alternatives. A father of a teenager offered the following example:

> My son borrowed $200 from me to finance a weekend trip with friends and to pay a speeding ticket. We worked out a payment plan that would involve his doing various jobs around the house, including mowing the yard and washing our family car. A couple of weeks passed, and he had not attempted to fulfill any of his contractual obligations to me. Yet he continued to want

to go out evenings and spend time and money with his friends. I was becoming more and more angry and decided that some intervention was necessary.

In the past, I would have said something like, "Until you first make an effort to pay me back, you're not going to go out tonight and spend money on yourself that you rightfully owe me! So, are you going to mow the yard this afternoon or not?" Instead, I said, "I think it's great that you are shooting some pool tonight with your friends. Before you go, would you rather mow the yard or wash the car?" He picked washing the car. I accomplished my goal, and he got to do what he wanted to do. Rather than either one of us feeling angry or manipulated by the other, it was a win/win deal for both of us.

A child with an unmet need for independence and freedom will seek power in one of three ways—through *confrontation*, through *revenge*, or through *avoidance behavior*. Each of these behaviors is a power-play, and parents can learn to identify each particular power play by examining how the child's behavior is making them feel.

Confrontation

By far, the most common expression of power-seeking is when a child becomes *confrontational*. The parent can recognize this power-play when the child's behavior results in the parent's feeling *angry*.

A favorite confrontation technique is "defiant compliance," whereby the child will do as told but not in the manner in which the adult wants it done. A parent shared this story:

> My teenage son and I used to have these enormous battles over my getting him to mow the yard. I would force the issue, and off he would go behind the lawnmower, furious over the fact that I had "won." Time after time, he would finish and drive off in his car, and I would discover that he had left a 10′ by 20′ strip of grass on the far side of the house that he had "forgotten" to mow.

In dealing with a confrontational child, parents must refrain from allowing themselves to lose their temper (which automatically gives their emotional power to their child). When a child is "pushing for more power" and a parent responds like an angry dictator, the parent only serves to impress the child with the value of power and increases the kid's desire to obtain it.

A good course of action is for the parent to disengage from the power struggle by offering her confrontational child an opportunity to engage in some mutual problem-solving. "Lindsey, we've got a problem here. I know that, together, you and I can solve it." Then, using the skills of communication and compromise, the parent has an opportunity to empower her child to become a part of the solution. This sort of problem-solving will require the parent and the child to examine together the range of choices that are available to them and is an excellent way to help a confrontational child feel respected and powerful.

Revenge

If an on-going power struggle makes a child feel like he is almost always being defeated by a parent, he may then resort to *revenge.* Children who seek revenge are convinced that they are not lovable, so they exert a sort of perverse power through making others feel as bad as they do. Parents can recognize this tactic if their child says something cruel that *hurts their feelings,* such as "I hate you! I wish you weren't my parents!"

This form of misbehavior presents a particularly difficult challenge. A parent who has been hurt by a child is tempted to retaliate, thereby establishing a revenge cycle between himself and his child that is enormously destructive to their relationship.

To help a vengeful child, parents must remember that the child's behavior stems from feelings of powerlessness and discouragement. Summoning up the maturity required of an adult, the parent should remain calm and avoid the temptation to retaliate or to hurt the kid back. By encouraging the child to express his feelings in private conversation, the parent can try to discover the cause of the child's pain and to address it in a caring, understanding manner.

A parent can also acknowledge the hurtful words and ask, "What can we do to make us both feel better?" In telling the child that her words are hurtful, and then inviting input from the child by asking, "What would you like to see happen so that you won't feel the need to use spiteful words?" the adult gives power to the child.

Above all, it is important to show goodwill and unconditional love and to make every effort to reestablish a caring, nurturing relationship with the child.

Avoidance Behavior

When a child feels like he can never "win" and is totally powerless and inadequate, he may simply give up and—instead of doing things for himself—try to "draw power" from others by getting them to assist him. This power play is called *avoidance behavior*, and it usually evokes feelings of *despair and pity* from the parent who feels sorry for her seemingly "helpless" child. It is a common tactic of an attention-deficit child. Having given up all expectations of ever succeeding, the child seeks to be excused from responsible behavior and attempts to keep others from expecting anything of him, too.

When asked to clean up his room, an avoidance-behaving child will keep coming up with excuses to get the parent to clean the room for him. For example, the child might say, "I can't do it. My stomach doesn't feel very good. And my foot is kinda hurting, too. Could you please, please, do it for me?" Drawing power from parents is a subtle way of exercising control over them.

In helping a young person who feels inadequate and exhibits avoidance behavior, parents must avoid the temptation to "do things for the child." Instead, we can break a difficult task into smaller, "do-able" pieces that the child can handle. Also, it is vital that we eliminate all criticism and focus instead on emphasizing the child's assets and strengths—encouraging any effort upon the part of the child to improve, no matter how insignificant that effort may appear to be. As we help a child to feel more competent, the child will feel increasingly powerful, and the avoidance behavior will disappear.

Jesus was well aware of the human need to exercise power. He was quick to make the distinction, however, between social/political power and personal power. Those who seek power through the acquisition of money and possessions and high political office chase false dreams. All those things are just "smoke and mirrors" and have no lasting value or meaning. Jesus was not interested in pursuing those empty goals. He possessed incomparable gifts of leadership, and, at one point in His life, was offered the opportunity to establish a reign of political power over all the world; but it was a temptation He emphatically refused.[2] On the other hand, Jesus was a huge proponent of *personal* power, and He tried to empower people to take charge of their lives and to make the sort of responsible decisions that make life joyous and fulfilling.

Jesus would work especially hard at reducing power struggles between Himself and His child and would look for opportunities for His child to exercise positive decision-making and to feel personally powerful.

Through listening to children, asking their opinions, eliminating all unnecessary elements from the power struggle, offering win-win solutions, and extending an offer to engage in mutual problem-solving, parents can help resolve conflict situations in a manner whereby children feel that they are valued and that their opinions and decisions are important.

As we treat kids as persons who deserve our respect, we will lessen conflicts and empower them to experience the power, independence, and freedom that every child needs and desires.

---

[1]   Luke 4:18.
[2]   Luke 4:5–8.

Dr. B. Glenn Wilkerson

Discussion Ideas

- It is difficult to know just how and when to grant age-appropriate power and independence to a child. Give an example of a situation when your child has wanted power that was not appropriate for her age.

- The Old Testament tells the story of a power struggle between King David and his beloved son Absalom. The young man wanted his father's throne. Their confrontation became violent and ended in tragedy (2 Samuel 18–19:4). What are tactics you can use in dealing with a power-seeking child that will help settle the confrontation peacefully and effectively?

- Give an example of giving power to a child by offering him a choice between two acceptable alternatives.

- Mutual problem-solving is a wonderful tool in working with a power-seeking child. Share an example.

Chapter 11

When You Are Despairing
Over Not Doing Enough...
(Dealing with a Rebellious Child)

These are rebellious people, deceitful children,
children unwilling to listen to the Lord's instruction
(Isaiah 30:9).

In addition to the need to feel loved and wanted and the need to feel powerful, the third primary human need is for life to be both meaningful and fun.

All of us want our lives to count for something. We want to engage in activities that we judge to be meaningful—activities that will touch our lives and the lives of others in a manner that makes a difference. We want to leave this world a better place for our having lived in it. And, along the way, we want to experience moments of recreation, good humor, and fun.

A common complaint of parents is that, for no apparent reason, their teenagers are non-communicative and sullen. "All Megan does is sit around and pout. If she does say anything, it's to criticize her brothers and sisters and us!" On the other hand, a common complaint among teenagers at home is: "I'm bored! Hanging around home is no fun!"

When children do not experience life as either meaningful or fun, they resort to *rebellion*. While they may not be consciously aware of their own motivations, rebellious behavior on the part of children is usually intended to convey one of two messages: "We never do anything as a family that takes into account what I am interested in," or, "Things are a little slow around this place, and I'm going to create a little diversion even if it is distressful to those around me." Rebellion is a negative attempt upon the part of children to make life more meaningful, interesting, and enjoyable.

While leading His followers on the most meaningful spiritual journey the world has ever witnessed, Jesus also made sure that they experienced a lot of fun together. One of the first recorded events in Jesus' adult years was a wedding He and His disciples attended in the town of Cana. I am guessing He was at the center of things, laughing with people, telling jokes, and really enjoying Himself. When the hosts ran out of wine, He produced more so that the good times would keep flowing. Being around Jesus was anything but boring. He enabled people to savor life's deepest meanings, and, at the same time, He kept it fun.

The job of the parent is the most difficult of all human endeavors. Even when parents are trying their best to provide for the physical well-being of their children, to communicate values, and to teach their children how to relate to other people, their children still may make them feel that "it's not enough." If a parent is trying hard to meet the needs of her child and is still made to feel guilty of being an incompetent parent, the child is probably engaged in rebellion, and the unmet need of the child is for life to be more meaningful and fun.

The most effective way to curb rebellious behavior is the tactic of prevention.

First of all, we can prevent some rebellious behavior by simply asking each child, "What do you want to do?" and then building some of the family's activities around the interests of each child. When there are competing interests, a child may willingly participate in another person's chosen event this Saturday if he knows that the family will accommodate his interests the following weekend. Taking the time and effort to plan family outings and games can make life more enjoyable and interesting for children and their parents.

Secondly, there must be some sort of "compassion gene" in the human brain, because young people need—and are excited by—projects that enable them to help others. Engaging in family projects that benefit other people makes life more meaningful to children. The Apostle Paul recognized the need to engage people in projects that provide an opportunity for them to be part of a cause larger than themselves. One of the churches Paul helped start was in Corinth. There was a lot of dissension in the church with members going out of their way to criticize and complain about each other. One way Paul addressed the problem was to encourage the people to take a weekly offering to help feed starving families back in Jerusalem.[1] Uniting people around a worthy cause helped stop some of the rebellious behavior. In helping individuals to find meaning in their lives, Paul addressed an unmet need.

A third way to prevent rebellious behavior is for parents to give themselves permission to loosen up and have fun with their children. A good sense of humor upon the part of parents is a wonderful thing to share with children. However, while it is appropriate for a parent to gently poke fun at himself, a basic rule for the use of humor in the family is that parents should never make fun of the children. When adults joke about a child's appearance or behavior, the child will interpret the humor as a "put-down."

At times, rebellion and confrontation can look a lot alike. The difference is that rebellion is caused by the unmet need for life to be meaningful and fun, while confrontation is caused by a child's need for more power and freedom. Parents can differentiate between the two by examining how the child's actions make them feel. If the parent feels guilty ("I'm not a competent parent or my child wouldn't be so unresponsive and sullen"), then the child probably is exhibiting rebellion. If the parent feels angry about the child's behavior, then the child is likely seeking power through initiating a confrontation (see pages 113-14). Once parents understand the nature of the misbehavior, they can address the unmet need that has prompted the child's actions.

When a parent is faced with rebellious behavior, the important thing is not to be defensive or to argue with the child. Real problem-solving never takes place when people are upset and engaged in conflict. The first task of the parent is to calm down the immediate situation. Speaking in a calm, normal-volume voice, the parent can respond with a statement like, "Johnny, your behavior (or words) are not helpful to me, to you, or to the rest of the family. Let's talk about your feelings. Why are you behaving like you are?" Once the situation has calmed down, the parent can ask for ideas from the rebellious child as to how home life can be made more meaningful and fun.

Here is how one mother handled her rebellious son:

Raymond strolled into the kitchen, grabbed a handful of cookies and a carton of milk out of the refrigerator, and sat down at the table to eat. His mother Charlotte entered the kitchen, took one look at Raymond, and started in on him. "Raymond, I have told you *not* to snack this time of the morning. You'll spoil your lunch! Besides that, please don't drink out of the milk carton. You're fifteen years old! How many times do I have to tell you to use a glass! And you know I always wash on Saturdays. Have you put your dirty clothes in the hamper?"

Raymond shot back, "Mother, all I ever hear around here is you telling me to do stuff. 'Raymond, do this.' 'Raymond, do that.' It's all work and no play around this place. I am bored to tears! Jimmy Smith's folks are taking him to the ballpark this afternoon. But, oh no, not us! All you want me to do is work. Who did you use as a slave around here before you and Dad had me?"

Charlotte's first reaction was one of defensiveness. She and her husband had always tried to do as much as they could for Raymond. They had taken him to church, had supported him by going to his basketball games, and had signed him up for summer recreation programs. Charlotte opened her mouth to argue with him but stopped, because the boy's words were also stirring some feelings of guilt. Was she expecting too much out of Raymond? Were they good parents to the boy? Were other parents doing more for their children?

Then she inwardly smiled and thought, What is it that I'm supposed to be asking myself now? Oh, yeah! "What is the unmet need of my child?" Let's see now. If Raymond is making me feel guilty in regard to my "not doing enough" as a parent, then this little number he's pulling on me is rebellion. And rebellious behavior is connected to the need *for life to be meaningful and fun.*

Charlotte turned to Raymond and said, "Your father was my slave before I had you. That's a big reason why your birth was the happiest day of his life! And, I'll tell you what, Raymond. If you think my milk carton demands are a little too much, let's do this. I'll buy a second carton of milk to put in the refrigerator. You take a pen and write a big "R" on it so we'll know which carton belongs to you, and it'll be yours to drink any way you want to drink it. And, by the way, I agree with you about the Smiths. Why don't we plan something fun for our family to do this afternoon after we've all completed our chores?"

As Charlotte turned to walk out of the room, she had another thought about Raymond: Maybe he would feel less bored if he had something meaningful to do that would divert his attention from himself. She considered for a moment and then turned back to him and said, "Raymond, I've got a great idea for next Saturday. I'd like for our whole family to go down to the Salvation Army shelter and serve some meals to the homeless."

Charlotte realized that she was dealing with a rebellious child. Therefore, instead of allowing herself to get upset and defensive because of his comments, she used a little bit of humor with Raymond. And, knowing that the best means of curbing rebellious behavior is the tactic of prevention, she agreed to plan a fun outing that afternoon with their family.

Charlotte also realized that children, just like adults, have a need to make a difference in this world. So, she went on to schedule a family event at the Salvation Army shelter that would give her children an opportunity to help needy people. Serving others would make life more meaningful for her kids.

Jesus took time to have fun with the people around Him. He took them fishing and shared meals with them. He also enabled them to find meaning in life through helping people who were hungry, sick, or grieving over the loss of a loved one. If Jesus had a child, He would avert rebellious behavior by having fun with His son and giving him an opportunity to find meaning in the service of other people.

[1]   1 Corinthians 16:1–3.

Discussion Ideas

- Which of your child's interests can be incorporated into your family's activities to prevent (or reduce) rebellious behavior?

- Describe a time when you and your kids participated in a service project that benefited other people. Was it a meaningful experience for your children?

- God expects us to be good stewards of His creation. What environmental causes can you and your children embrace that will help keep the earth clean and beautiful? (For example, some families spend one Saturday morning a month walking together with trash bags, picking up paper and bottles in their neighborhood.)

- Name some fun activities that you and your children enjoy sharing together.

THE MISBEHAVIOR CHART
"What is the unmet need of the child?"

If the child's actions seem to say...	If you feel...	Then you are probably dealing with...	Whose unmet need is...	What can you do?
"Look at me!" "Listen to me!"	annoyed or frustrated	an <u>attention-seeking</u> child	the need for love and a sense of belonging	• If possible, do not reward demands for negative attention. • Encourage the child to examine his behavior and make better choices. • Surprise the child by giving her attention in ways that are unexpected. • "Catch her doing good" and give attention to that behavior.
1. "You can't make me do anything!" "I'll show you!" 2. "You never let me win!" "I can be as mean and cruel as you!" 3. "I am completely helpless and am not to be held responsible for anything."	1. angry 2. hurt 3. pity	a power-seeking child 1. who seeks power through <u>confrontation</u> 2. who seeks power through <u>revenge</u> 3. who seeks power through <u>avoidance behavior</u>	the need to have more power and control over his life	1. Listen to the child. Avoid unnecessary rules. Invite mutual problem-solving. Offer "win-win" solutions. 2. Do not punish or hurt back. Use empathy to understand the cause of the child's pain. Acknowledge the hurtful words and ask, "What can we do to make us both feel better?" 3. Continue to show goodwill. Avoid doing for the child. Arrange small successes. Encourage any effort the child makes to improve.
"I am so bored!" "I hate hanging around this place with you." "Why can't we do things and have some fun?"	guilty	a <u>rebellious</u> child	the need for life to be meaningful and fun	• Make rules that are reasonable and don't have too many of them. • Use a sense of humor; play games. • Have family outings and projects.

PART IV

Applying Jesus' Teachings

Chapter 12

When You Want to Rally the Troops...
(Conducting Family Meetings)

God is building a home. He's using us all—irrespective of how we got here—in what He is building....Now He's using you, fitting you in brick by brick, stone by stone, with Christ Jesus as the cornerstone that holds all the parts together (Ephesians 2:21–22).

Most families operate best as "controlled democracies"—with the parents functioning as the chief executive officers. In democracies, everyone owns a piece of the decision-making process and is made to feel that their opinions and contributions are important. One effective way of accomplishing the family's democratic goals is through a regular convening of family meetings.

Jesus once looked at His followers sitting around Him and said, "These people are my mother and my brothers."[1] He counted as "family" all those with whom he spent life's most intimate moments—those with whom He walked, talked, ate, and prayed. And He convened His family regularly to share thoughts and ideas and to discuss plans. His family gatherings often took place at meal-time where they talked about the events of the day, laughed together, and shared stories.

Family meetings should be fun experiences and can begin when the children are in elementary school. Their purpose is to help family members bond together, celebrate their successes, support each other during challenging times, solve problems, and organize busy schedules.

Family meetings reduce the intensity of the parent-child power struggle, because they enable everyone to be heard and to express their thoughts and feelings. As chores are distributed and recreational activities are planned, children feel empowered when their opinions are considered, along with those of their parents. Older youth are much more likely to adhere to the rules and to accept the consequences when those rules are broken, if they have been given an opportunity to help determine those rules and consequences. Family meetings provide parents and children a forum for settling conflicts, for giving encouragement, and for expressing positive feelings toward one another.

If possible, family gatherings should be scheduled at a regular time each week, so that everyone can adjust their plans accordingly. Members who are absent must honor the agreements established for that week. The meeting should begin on time and end on time, with the length of the meeting taking into account the age and attention span of the children. A good rule of thumb is to have meetings of fifteen minutes or less with younger children and not more than thirty minutes with older ones.

Some families share the leadership of the meetings with the older children, with a parent taking charge of the first couple of sessions, so that the children will see how it is done before they lead a meeting.

Family meetings should be opened on a positive note. For example, each person can be asked to share "one thing they like about the family" or "the best thing that happened to them this past week."

Everyone needs to be encouraged to contribute to the discussion. In the first few meetings, parents can allow their children to talk and make some suggestions before they jump in with their parental suggestions; otherwise, the children may conclude that the meetings are merely an exercise in fake democracy. And since "yes or no" votes tend to establish winners and losers, every attempt should be made to help all members come to a general agreement. When an issue that escapes general agreement arises, it can be put aside for the next week's meeting. If an issue requires immediate attention, and a quick decision cannot be reached, the parent can resolve the dilemma with a temporary solution: "Something needs to be done right away, but we don't appear ready to make a decision. So, I will decide the course of action for now, and we can review the situation again next week."

Often, when family members disagree on a subject, they will be willing to go along with what others want to do as long as they feel like what they want to do will also be honored. For example, if the family is discussing where to go for a family outing, Raul may be okay with his sister Maria's suggestion that the family go to the beach this Saturday if everybody agrees with his suggestion to see a movie the following Saturday. Family meetings are a good, safe place for children to practice "give-and-take" skills.

Whatever is important to members is "fair game" for discussion, and the children's issues should be given equal attention, along with those expressed by the adults. One good practice is to use "I-messages" when communicating feelings. When we say, "I feel so angry when you...," it comes across much less threatening and invites a friendlier response than does the same message phrased in terms of, "You make me so angry when you...."

Another helpful tool in family meetings is a sense of humor, and the meetings should concentrate just as much on planning family fun as they do on assigning tasks and solving problems. Some families end their meetings by playing a game.

During family meetings, careful attention should be given to pinpointing the real issues. Often, "the problem is not the problem." For example, the real point of contention may not be where the family goes out to eat so much as who decides where the family goes to eat. If the real issue is a matter of power, it can be pointed out in a friendly, nonjudgmental manner: "It appears that we all want to get our own way. How can we resolve this?" The meetings should not become gripe sessions. A rule can be established that complaints will be heard only if the complainer is willing to help seek a solution.

During a family meeting, the parents should take time to clarify and summarize what has been discussed. Then they can ask for a commitment to what has been agreed upon. For example, they can say, "We decided that everybody is going to take turns carrying out the trash. Does everyone understand it that way, and are we all willing to honor this decision until the next meeting?" The agreements that are reached are to be in effect until the next meeting. If a child does not honor the agreement, the parents can apply natural and logical consequences. And agreements of real importance can be recognized in the form of a written contract.

An example of a simple written contract might be as follows:

> Jeremy is to have full use of his car, which his parents bought for him. He is to pay for his gas. As owners of the car, his parents will cover the cost of the car's insurance. While Jeremy is driving the car, speeding and the use of alcohol are strictly prohibited and will result in Jeremy's loss of his car privileges for a month. All parties trust Jeremy to use good judgment in the use of the car.

Both Jeremy and his parents sign and date the contract. Then if any violations occur, there is no question as to the nature of the consequences.

Every family should have a meeting to establish a few basic rules concerning group interaction. For example, one critical rule might be that no physical or emotional abuse is permitted. Everyone in the family must follow the rules, and older children who choose not to do so must make living arrangements elsewhere. No one is kicked out of the house. Those who choose not to adhere to the rules are making the choice to leave. If that is their decision, they go with the family's love, and, if and when they choose to follow the rules, they are lovingly welcomed back into the household. Enforcing both the rules and the resulting consequences is not spiteful; it is a loving option that must be exercised by responsible adults for the protection of the entire family. No individual should be given the power to terrorize other family members with physical or emotional abuse. The family meeting can help ensure that the home is a safe, loving refuge where all members are treated with dignity and respect.

Family meetings, at their best, are governed by the spirit of love modeled by Jesus. His willingness to listen, understand, and deeply care for others are the bricks that form the house that God would have us construct. For the family to provide that sort of spiritual security for one another, they must gather on a regular basis to talk. As the Psalmist said, "Those who watch for my life [should] consult together"[2]

The family meeting can teach children the art of compromise and delayed gratification and can be an important means of giving each and every member of the family a sense of being valued, accepted, and understood. It is a powerful tool for the development of our children's self-esteem.

Jesus' family was His disciples. He regularly convened them to teach, to correct, and to encourage. It worked beautifully with His disciples, and He would make it work for His children as well.

---

[1]   Mark 3:34–35.
[2]   Psalm 71:10.

Discussion Ideas

- Describe the decision-making process in the family in which you were raised. Were children involved in the decision-making?

- Every family should have a meeting to establish a few basic rules concerning group interaction. What might some of those rules be?

- Jesus' spiritual "family" consisted of His twelve disciples. Many of their meetings were convened over a meal. Do you have regular family meals? What is accomplished by having family meals?

- While the parents are the "chief executive officers" in a democratic family, everyone in the family is given equal respect and dignity. Would you call your family a democratic family? If not, describe how your family operates.

Chapter 13

When You Feel Like
You Cannot Take Much More...
(Dealing with Anger Issues)

Everyone should be quick to listen, slow to speak and slow to become angry, for man's anger does not bring about the righteous life that God desires (James 1:19–20).

To discipline children in a manner that reflects love for them, adults must learn how to deal appropriately with their own anger. Like all human emotions, anger itself is neither good nor bad. It simply *is*. Anger is often justified. It becomes destructive only when it is directed or expressed inappropriately. Learning how to deal with our anger in a positive way is important. Or, as the Bible says, "In your anger do not sin."[1]

When Jesus saw the money changers cheating poor people in the temple, He became angry. However, He did not come to blows with any of the perpetrators. He simply went about destroying and scattering the apparatus they were using to cheat. He also raised His voice against their crimes.[2]

Like Jesus, responsible adults work at controlling their temper and expressing it in an appropriate manner. Whenever we express our anger inappropriately with our children, we always lose. A father commented:

> My son can really manipulate those situations when he and I get into a confrontation. When I'm lecturing him over something he has done, he'll say something disrespectful to me, and I'll lose my temper. When that happens, the attention is immediately shifted from him and his misbehavior and is focused back on me. He feels wronged by the fact that I blew up at him, and whatever moral instruction I had hoped to impart is now lost on him.

The power to control our own destiny is an important aspect of being mature, responsible adults. No one can "make us" lose our temper. We allow people to push our emotional buttons. When parents allow their children to manipulate their emotions (including anger) and then react inappropriately, they are handing over their emotional power to their kids.

A very real danger of inappropriately expressed anger is its potential for violence. Violent behavior often is passed from generation to generation. Some studies indicate that people who were abused as children are four to six times more likely to abuse their own children than are parents from nonabusive homes.[3] [4] According to the Child Abuse Prevention Network, over eighty percent of prisoners who have been jailed for violent crimes were abused as children.[5] Those who suffered physical abuse when they were young must be especially careful not to pass the habit of violence on to their own children.

Even the types of family violence are often repeated. Without realizing what they are doing, people will copy their parent's behaviors that they hated the most when they themselves were children. An example is a man who comes home from a hard day of work, pours himself a drink, picks up the newspaper, and sinks into an easy chair to relax. His two-year-old comes in, wanting her father's attention. When her father does not respond, she becomes more insistent in her demands for attention. The father loses patience and reaches over and slaps the child on her behind. If she is a strong-willed child, she may refuse to cry or to acknowledge the reprimand, and the irritating behavior may continue. The father next reacts with two more blows on the bottom...then three, and, finally, in a fit of rage, he picks the child up by a leg and throws her onto the couch. While immediately horrified and ashamed over what he has done, the dad has simply repeated the same parenting behaviors that his father used with him.

Parents must be very intentional if they are to change long-established patterns of family violence. One of the most important promises a parent can make to himself and to God is: "I will not touch my child when I am angry." Anger is the primary culprit in irrational, aggressive behavior. When anger is absent, physical touch is not likely to be violent.

Anger-management techniques are a proven way to help change the way adults express their anger. Among those techniques are the following:

Take a parent's time-out.

If an adult does become angry, some physical separation from the child is important. The adult can say, "I need a 'parent's time-out.' Please go to your room. I will come and get you in twenty minutes, and we will continue our discussion." While many well-intentioned parents spank their children, it is important to remember that Jesus never raised his hand against another human being. Current research shows that children who are regularly spanked are twice as likely to engage in violent behavior when they grow older.[6] If you feel like spanking your child, take a parent's time out and consider other forms of discipline. (See Chapter 14, "When It Comes Time to Discipline".)

And, in the case of parents who do decide to spank, a parent's time-out is important so that any anger is allowed to diminish before any physical punishment is administered. Again, the primary rule to follow is: *we should never touch our children when we are angry.*

Engage in some physical exercise.

Physical activity is an appropriate and effective way of dealing with our anger. Aerobic exercise, in particular, can be helpful. It causes the body to produce endorphins, a "pleasure chemical," which exerts a soothing, calming influence. A prominent psychiatrist said:

> I believe that some sort of physical expression is critical as a means of expressing anger appropriately. Some people jog or take a brisk walk to reduce tension.
>
> As for me, when I feel anger and tension building up inside, I tie a knot in one end of a bath towel. Then I go to my bedroom, close the door, and get on my knees by the side of my bed.
>
> I grasp the loose end of the towel with both hands, and, swinging it from above my head like a club, I spend two or three minutes yelling and beating the dickens out of my bed. Not only does it exhaust me physically; it also helps me to harmlessly release my pent-up feelings.

It is important that each of us finds a harmless way of physically expressing our anger and then teach these techniques to our children.[7]

Practice relaxation skills.

Taking slow, deep breaths can be helpful. In addition to having a calming effect, slow, deep breathing for thirty seconds also increases the production of endorphins.

Talk through the feelings.

If angry feelings toward someone persist over a period of time, it is often helpful to share those feelings with a trusted confidante (counselor, pastor, or friend) who will listen with empathy and without judgment. Talking about our angry feelings is like putting ice cubes in hot water—it helps dissipate the heat.

Discover the underlying reason for the anger.

In many instances, anger is a product of fear. We become angry, for example, because we are afraid of feeling embarrassed, appearing ignorant, or not being given proper respect. When we get angry, a good question to ask ourselves is: "What am I afraid of?" When we deal with that fear, the anger will diminish or go away.

We are responsible for our own emotional responses, including the manner in which we express anger. Those who have been its victims are not condemned to pass violence on as a family legacy. By exercising insight, courage, and forgiveness, we can free ourselves from parenting behaviors that have been handed down for generations. The effective disciplining of our children's behavior begins with learning how to discipline our own behavior as Jesus did. The good news is that, when we employ new behaviors for dealing with anger that are based on unconditional love, we will establish new parenting patterns for our children and their children for generations to come.

[1] Psalm 4:4.

[2] Matthew 21:12–13.

[3] William A. Check, *Child Abuse*. Chelsea House, 1989, p. 44.

[4] Katie D. Koster, ed., *Child Abuse: Opposing Viewpoints*. Greenhaven Press, 1994, p. 119.

[5] "Child Abuse Fact Sheet," Prepared by the Houston Chapter of the Child Abuse Prevention Network. December 1992.

[6] Alice Park, "The Long-Term Effects of Spanking," Time Magazine, May , 2010, http://content.time.com/time/magazine/article/0,9171,1983895,00.html

[7] Dr. Grace Weimerskirch, interview, April 20, 1981.

Discussion Ideas

- When was the last time you witnessed an adult expressing anger inappropriately? How did the person act?

- Why is it important to avoid touching someone when you are angry?

- When the Psalmist says, "Be angry, and do not sin" (Psalm 4:4), he is encouraging his listeners not to express their anger through violence. Is physical violence ever justified when we get angry? Explain your answer.

- How do you "let off steam" when you feel angry?

Chapter 14

When It Comes Time to Discipline...

Moreover, we have all had human fathers [and mothers] who disciplined us and we respected them for it.... No discipline seems pleasant at the time, but painful. Later on, however, it produces a harvest of righteousness and peace for those who have been trained by it (Hebrews 12:9, 11).

A great social upheaval is in the process of taking place. Rather than viewing people as disposable cogs in a social machine, this cultural revolution proclaims the value of the individual person. Proponents of the movement tout it as exciting and new. It is exciting...but it is not new. It is simply a reflection of the teachings of Jesus regarding the sanctity of each and every individual as a child of God. My response is: "It's about time!"

Beginning in the West and spreading rapidly among other cultures, the issue of "human rights" has become a matter of international concern. This perception of humans—as beings of infinite worth—is the product of a long evolution of cultural and religious hopes and ideas. It has become an important element of human expectation to the extent that even children today expect their personhood to be honored and respected.

Therefore, the old authoritarian parenting models of punishment and reward—based on the idea of dominant parents and submissive children—do not fare well within the modern family system. Rudolf Dreikurs has provided some marvelous insights for those of us who are deeply concerned about the quality of our relationships with our children. Dr. Dreikurs says:

> We must realize the futility of trying to impose our will upon our children. No amount of punishment will bring about lasting submission. Today's children are willing to take any amount of punishment in order to assert their "rights." Confused and bewildered parents mistakenly hope that punishment will *eventually* bring results, without realizing that they are actually getting nowhere with their methods. At best, they gain only temporary results from punishment. When the same punishment has to be repeated again and again, it should be obvious that it does not work.[1]

Likewise, the "rewards" system has its drawbacks as a means of compelling appropriate behavior in our children. Rewarding good behavior with money, privileges, and "things" teaches our children to think only in terms of "what's in it for me?" and robs them of the satisfaction of being a responsible, contributing member of the family. Our children sense that we only punish and reward those whom we feel are "inferior" to us, so our children react to both models with resentment and reluctant compliance. Both the "punishment" and the "rewards" models for influencing behavior indicate a lack of respect for the personhood of our children.

The word "punishment" infers that a child has to suffer to learn, while the word "discipline" means "to teach." Parents who make the decision to discipline rather than to punish their children are constantly asking themselves the question, "What lesson do I want to teach my child?" A very useful and democratic model for disciplining children is a system built upon "natural and logical consequences." The use of natural and logical consequences is a teaching tool that encourages children to engage in responsible, appropriate behaviors.

Natural Consequences

"Natural consequences" are produced by the natural flow of events with very little interference from adults. For example, if Martha refuses to eat her dinner, she does not eat that evening. She is not allowed to substitute snacks in place of eating her dinner. "Going to bed hungry" is not a cruel or unusual punishment; it is the natural consequence of not eating one's food. The resulting hunger pangs will not pose any sort of health hazard for a normal, healthy child and may serve to teach the child to take better responsibility for eating when food is provided at mealtimes.

The Bible gives us numerous examples of natural consequences caused by people's irresponsible behavior. Noah got drunk and totally embarrassed himself with his sons.[2] Amnon (King David's son) raped his sister Tamar, which resulted in their brother Absalom's hating Amnon.[3] Natural consequences are the natural result of bad behavior.

Allowing natural consequences to take place, with little or no intervention upon the part of the parent, will require some thought and self-discipline. It is natural for a parent to want to swoop in and immediately apply disciplinary measures when he sees his child disobey or misbehave. Often, however, a greater lesson is taught by the consequences that are the natural outcome of irresponsible or unwise decisions. A child who is warned not to drink vinegar, and who proceeds to do so in direct contravention of her parent's instructions, will probably make that mistake only once.

Logical Consequences

Sometimes, however, the natural consequences of a misdeed are inappropriate or dangerous to a child's well-being. For example, the natural consequence of a child playing in the street is that she will be injured by a passing car. In such cases, parents can institute "logical consequences"—circumstances "structured" by adults as a logical response to a child's inappropriate behavior. One logical consequence of a child edging toward the street might be that, without a big fuss, she is firmly picked up by her parent, carried inside the house, and told, "Since you are choosing not to play in the yard, you must play inside. Maybe you can go outside again tomorrow and play safely." Another example of a logical consequence would be the case where Billy leaves his clothes lying on the floor, and his mother does not do his laundry because "there's nothing in the hamper to wash."

The difference between a natural consequence and a logical consequence can be illustrated by the following example. A mother said:

> We have a Spanish-speaking housekeeper who comes to clean our house once a week. She is one of those persons who like to throw things away. We don't speak enough Spanish to make it clear to her what to throw away and what to keep. So, she just throws away everything that she finds loose on the counters or on the floors.
>
> After Maria's second week of working for us, our kids started picking up everything on their bedroom floors and countertops the night before she comes to work. We don't have to say anything to them anymore about cleaning up their rooms.

The story is a great example of how natural consequences can encourage desired behavior. On the other hand, if the maid spoke English, the parents could have structured the same learning experience by *telling* her to throw away everything she found on the bedroom floors and countertops, thereby encouraging desired behavior through the creation of a logical consequence.

A good illustration of a logical consequence was a practice instituted by a parent regarding curfew:

> My son and I discussed his curfew situation and agreed that each ten minutes that he comes in past curfew, he must come home one hour earlier the next time he goes out. So if he comes in twenty minutes late, his curfew is lowered by two hours at his next outing. I don't have to yell at him anymore for breaking curfew. The logical consequence takes care of the situation.

Establishing logical consequences can give parents an opportunity to exercise real creativity in structuring learning opportunities for their children. For example, in cases where a child neglects to perform one of his chores, a logical consequence might be that he cannot go to his next desired activity until that job has been completed: "I'm sorry you have chosen not to make your bed. You'll have to wait to ride your bicycle to the park with your friends until the bed is made."

Family meetings offer wonderful opportunities to discuss logical consequences for poor behavior/choices. To be effective, logical consequences should follow the "4 R's."[4] Logical consequences:

- are *respectful* of the child;
- are *related* to the child's mistake (if the child makes a mess, she cleans it up);
- are *reasonable* and age-appropriate (they are not so excessive that they are viewed as punishment rather than as a means of repairing the mistake); and
- are aimed at teaching the child to take *responsibility* for his mistake.

Adults must be sure that logical consequences are not viewed as a form of disguised punishment or revenge. One key is to give careful thought toward making certain that the structured consequence is an appropriate response to inappropriate behavior. Also, the less parents talk about "consequences," the less the consequences will appear to be a punishment. Rather than being accompanied by a lecture, logical consequences should be applied with minimal discussion.

One father shared this story:

Our seven-year-old daughter is a "night person."
We battle with her every evening over going to bed,

and then every morning over getting up in time to catch her carpool to school. One morning, she refused to get up, and, consequently, missed her ride. Instead of my wife or me taking her to school (as we have done in the past), we decided to implement a logical consequence in response to her irresponsible behavior. We sat her down at the breakfast table, and I told her, "Darling, it's our job to provide you a ride to school every morning. I'm sorry that you chose to stay up late last night and overslept and missed your ride. Now, it's *your* job to find a way for you to get to school. Let's write on a piece of paper the choices that you have."

I got a piece of paper and wrote, "Walk." Then she took the paper and wrote, "Ride." I said, "That's a good option. Since you've missed the ride I provided for you, why don't you give me the names of some of your friends, and I'll dial their telephone numbers so you can ask their parents if they can give you a ride?"

She said, "That won't work. I guess we better start walking."

The subsequent mile-and-a-half walk to school (with me accompanying her on my bicycle) has had the happy result of her now going to bed earlier and getting up on time with only minimal protest. I'm pretty sure, however, that the reason she received that walk to school as a learning experience—rather than perceiving it as a punishment—was that she understood it to be a logical consequence of her irresponsible behavior.

A frequent question at parent workshops is, "How can I apply logical consequences when immediate disciplinary action is needed to correct my child's extreme misbehavior, like throwing a tantrum or hitting another child?" In lieu of spanking, the American Academy of Pediatrics recommends the use of "time-outs"—isolating the child from contact with anyone else and giving the child a chance to calm down and to choose more appropriate behaviors.[5]

The use of time-outs as a logical consequence of misbehavior is accomplished, when things are calm and no emotions are involved, by the parent and child mutually agreeing upon a time-out place. As to how long a child should spend in time-out, a good rule of thumb is "one minute of time-out per each year of the child's chronological age."

Many parents employ a variation of time-out called the "self-quieting technique." The child is told, "Go to your time-out place, think about your behavior, and come out when you have calmed down and feel like you can relate to your sister in a quiet, caring manner." The responsibility for appropriate behavior is thereby given to the child. It was a technique Jesus frequently used, calling people to examine their inappropriate behaviors and to make better choices.

A key to successfully applying logical consequences concerns the manner in which they are delivered to the child. While remaining firm and uncompromising, parents must maintain a calm, respectful, and affirming attitude when enforcing the logical consequences of irresponsible behavior. Children are quick to respond negatively whenever they detect vengeful motives. An unemotional response by their parents allows children to learn from the consequence rather than to become angry and to get involved in power struggles. For example, instead of angrily saying to Marcus, "I *told* you that you couldn't go out until you washed the dishes!" a parent (utilizing a pleasant, nonjudgmental voice) could say, "I'm sorry that your chores aren't completed. I know that you'll take care of them so that you can go out." This approach in imposing a logical consequence is neither spiteful nor demeaning. It instead offers encouragement and indicates an implied trust and confidence in Marcus's ability to "take care of things."

Children usually can see the justice of appropriate consequences and will accept them. A consistent application of natural and logical consequences, therefore, often results in a remarkable reduction of friction and an amazing increase in family harmony.

Jesus was a master at helping people to understand the natural and logical consequences of their irresponsible or inappropriate behavior. One of His favorite disciplinary—or teaching—tools was storytelling. An example is His "Parable of the Rich Fool."[6] Jesus described a man who dedicated his life to accumulating wealth and possessions and who then suddenly died without having a chance to enjoy them. He said, "The man's possessions will now pass on to someone else. How foolish it is to spend your time on this earth in a selfish pursuit of treasures instead of trying to discover God's purpose for your life and striving to serve that purpose." In pointing out that the natural consequence of a selfish "me-first" existence is a meaningless, unfulfilled life, Jesus was inviting His listeners to make a decision in regard to the values that would define their lives.

Jesus disciplined His followers through the use of natural and logical consequences that helped them to learn from their mistakes and to make responsible choices and decisions. He would do the same with His child.

[1] Rudolf Driekurs, *Children: the Challenge*. Penguin Books, 1987, p. 69.
[2] Genesis 9:21–23.
[3] 2 Samuel 13:10–22.
[4] Kathryn J. Kvols, Redirecting Children's Misbehavior Workbook, INCAP Publications, 1993, p. 43.
[5] Alice Park, "The Long-Term Effects of Spanking," Time Magazine, May , 2010, http://content.time.com/time/magazine/article/0,9171,1983895,00.html
[6] Luke 12:16-21.

Discussion Ideas

- Allowing a child to accept the natural consequences of her irresponsible actions is crucial to her becoming a responsible adult. What are some examples of natural consequences that can and should be left for the child to address?

- The Old Testament writers talked a great deal about the Israelites bringing calamities upon themselves as a result of their bad behavior. It is important that we help our child understand that irresponsible behavior can bring bad consequences. In talking with toddlers, how would you describe the natural consequences of touching a hot stove or playing in the street? Or with teens, the natural consequences of promiscuous sex and drug abuse?

- Describe a time when you successfully used a logical consequence to help your child behave more responsibly.

- Share an example of stating a logical consequence in such a manner that it is not viewed as a "disguised punishment."

Chapter 15

When You Are Instilling Responsibility...

> *When Joseph's master heard the words that the master's wife spoke to him, saying, "This is the way your servant treated me," he became enraged. And Joseph's master took him and put him into the prison, the place where the king's prisoners were confined; he remained there in prison. But the LORD was with Joseph and showed him steadfast love; he gave him favor in the sight of the chief jailer. The chief jailer committed to Joseph's care all the prisoners who were in the prison, and whatever was done there, he was the one who did it. The chief jailer paid no heed to anything that was in Joseph's care (Genesis 40:19–23).*

Joseph is one of the Bible's best examples of the connection between responsibility and freedom. When he was falsely accused and put in prison in Egypt, Joseph responded by taking on duties and helping the chief jailer. As a result, Joseph ended up being given free run of the prison. His willingness to take on responsibility was his ticket to freedom.

In helping children develop a sense of responsibility, it is important that we enable them to understand that the more responsible they become, the more freedom they will enjoy.

It is all a matter of trust. The more responsibly Felicia behaves, the more her parents will trust her, and, the more they trust her, the more freedom they will give her. On the other hand, if Felicia abuses her freedom through irresponsible choices, the logical consequence will be the removal or reduction of some of her privileges. That is how children learn that personal freedom is the product of responsible behavior—and that lack of freedom is the result of irresponsible behavior.

Adults need to allow children to learn from their mistakes. I am not talking about dangerous or life-threatening mistakes—just the normal mistakes that kids make when they are growing up. When we become overly protective in shielding our children from the consequences of their poor choices and mistakes, we deny them valuable learning experiences that can teach self-discipline and responsibility. It is a lesson taught me by my son Kevin.

Like many kids who are attention-deficit, Kevin is very bright. His junior year in high school, he started out in all college preparatory classes, but, by the end of the first six weeks, he was dropped from every one of them and was sent to regular classes. The problem was with his homework assignments. He would forget to bring them home. Or, if he brought his homework home, he would forget to do it. Or, if he did his homework, he would forget to take it back to school. Or, if he did take it back to school, he would leave it in his locker and forget to take it to class. He could listen in class and make straight *A*'s on the tests. But when you mix in a string of zeroes on homework, you end up with a *C* or *D* grade average. It drove me nuts. So, I was constantly on him, reminding him about his schoolwork. In fact, we argued about it all the time. Finally, I took him to see a psychiatrist about his "problem."

I told the psychiatrist what was happening, and I finished by saying, "Doctor, fix him!"

The psychiatrist was quiet for a bit, and then he said, "Whose problem is this anyway?" And both he and my son Kevin looked at *me!*

I thought for a moment and then replied, "I guess I have made it mine."

The psychiatrist said, "You and your son both agree that your nagging him about his grades is hurting your relationship. Also, the nagging doesn't seem to be improving your son's academic performance. Maybe you are going to have to make a choice between maintaining the relationship or continuing to be 'in charge' of your son's grades. If you had to choose between the two, what would your choice be?"

I instantly replied, "I'll take the relationship, of course." I said, "Kevin, I'll make sure you have a quiet, private place in which to study. Your homework responsibility is now yours."

What the therapist did was to help me place the responsibility back where it belonged—which was with my son. Our relationship immediately improved. And, as Kevin began to deal with the natural consequences of poor grades (such as removal from honors classes, flunking a course, etc.), he became increasingly more responsible and self-disciplined. In fact, he went on to get a college degree and is a very successful businessman today.

My experience in that psychiatrist's office was, for me, a tremendous life lesson. I had been preaching unconditional love every Sunday, but the love I was showing Kevin was very conditional. Our conversations almost always revolved around his academic achievements and how disappointed I was in his performance. How hypocritical! The doctor placed two options on a plate, handed them to me, and invited me to make a choice: Will I love Kevin for who he *is*...or will I love him for what he *does*? That office visit was one of the greatest spiritual growth experiences in my life.

Allowing a child to make noncritical mistakes and to experience the resulting consequences is a very difficult yet loving thing for a caring adult to do. Because we want our children to live pain-free lives, some parents even lie for their kids—and make excuses and cover up for them at school—to keep them from getting into trouble. We need to remember that when our children are allowed to experience the consequences of their mistakes, they learn to make more responsible choices in the future. And, as they make good choices, they discover that being a responsible person opens the doors to personal freedom.

Jesus practiced what behavioral psychologists today call the doctrine of "the excellent mistake." If a person engages in a behavior that is not productive, quits the behavior, and uses the experience as a learning opportunity—that is an excellent mistake. Thomas Edison reportedly performed more than a thousand experiments trying to invent the light bulb. When he was asked how he could keep going after making so many mistakes, he replied, "What mistakes? Each time I'm just learning what doesn't work, bringing me closer to what does work." Edison's excellent mistakes eventually led him to success with his creation of the light bulb in 1879. Helping children understand that they are going to be loved and valued in spite of their mistakes allows them to take on new responsibilities and to explore new freedoms without fear of failure.

If a person acted irresponsibly or made a mistake, Jesus did not beat the person down verbally or make him feel bad about himself. He would offer forgiveness, point out the learning opportunities inherent in the mistake, and encourage the person to make wiser choices in the future. "That was an excellent, not-to-be-repeated mistake. What did you learn from it? What are you going to do differently in the future?"

Then, when people began to act more responsibly, Jesus would entrust them with additional responsibility. He would do the same with His child.

Another way to help kids become responsible persons is for parents to lay aside their own feelings of shame and failure when they see their children make mistakes. How many times have you been at the grocery store and have seen a cranky kid slapped and yanked around by an embarrassed parent who did not handle the situation properly? If we allow ourselves to feel embarrassed over our child's behavior, we are liable to overreact and to impose punishments and restrictions that go far beyond the bounds of natural and logical consequences. The child then feels unjustly wronged, and, as a result, misses the learning opportunity that the situation could have provided. For example, when a child misbehaves in a store, a logical consequence would be for the parent to take the child outside and say, "We do not yell and run up and down the aisles in a store. Can you behave better now, or do we need to go home?" Then we must be sure to follow through by leaving the store and going home if the child continues to misbehave.

I love the story of the woman in a grocery store who happened upon a grandpa and his poorly behaving three-year-old grandson. It was obvious that Gramps had his hands full with the kid screaming for candy in the candy aisle, cookies in the cookie aisle, and the same for fruit, cereal, and soda. Meanwhile, Gramps was working his way around the store, saying in a controlled voice, "'Easy, Albert, we won't be long—easy, boy."

Another outburst, and she heard Gramps calmly say, "It's okay, Albert, just a couple of more minutes and we'll be outta here—hang in there." At the checkout, the little terror was throwing items out of the cart, and Gramps again in a controlled voice said, "Albert, Albert, relax buddy, don't get upset. We'll be home in five minutes; stay cool, Albert."

Very impressed, the woman went outside where Gramps was loading his groceries and the boy into the car. She said, "You know, sir, it's none of my business, but you were amazing in there. I don't know how you did it. That whole time you kept your composure, and no matter how loud and disruptive the boy got, you just calmly kept saying things would be okay. Albert is very lucky to have you for his grandpa."

"Thanks, lady," said the old man, "but I'm Albert—the little brat's name is Mikey."

Gramps provides a good example of an adult's not feeling embarrassed or overreacting to his child's public misbehavior. He made a mistake, however, in allowing the misbehavior to continue. He should have taken the child to a quiet place in the store where they could talk privately for a few moments and said, "Mikey, you are not allowed to behave badly at the store. I know you are bored. We're going to finish my shopping, and then I'll take you over to the toy section where we can try out some of the new toys together." Or, Gramps could have escorted the boy to the car and said, "Because you did not behave well, we're leaving the store and going home. Maybe we'll try again tomorrow." Even three-year-olds can be taught responsible behavior.

Another way of transferring responsibility to our children is through having family meetings. When children—especially older kids—are brought into the family decision-making process, their movement toward independence and responsible adulthood is made much easier.

If young people help determine the rules and the consequences for breaking those rules, they can only blame themselves when they must be disciplined. They are, therefore, taught one of the basic truths of adult living: we must take responsibility for our own actions and choices. And, as children prove themselves to be more and more responsible, they can be handed a greater and greater role in making decisions regarding their own lives. Through this process, children learn that mature, adult living is a combination of both responsibility and freedom.

Jesus told a story about a rich man who left the country on a business trip.[1] Since he was going to be away for a long time, the man gave large amounts of money to three of his employees to invest on his behalf while he was gone. He gave one employee five talents ($1,250,000), a second employee two talents ($450,000), and a third employee one talent ($225,000)—each according to his abilities.[2] When the wealthy man returned home, he discovered that the first two men had worked hard at doubling their employer's money, and he rewarded them appropriately. Meanwhile, the third man had not done a thing with his money. The businessman was upset with the third man and took his talent away from him and gave it to the first man; it was a logical consequence of irresponsible behavior.

The point of Jesus' story is clear: if a person acts responsibly, he will be entrusted with additional responsibility and freedom. And, if a person acts irresponsibly, he will have his freedoms reduced.

One of Jesus' gifts to His child would be to help her learn to accept responsibility and to make wise decisions regarding the freedom that He gave her. As she grew in her ability to act responsibly, He would entrust her with additional freedom. His goal would be to see her mature into a responsible adult who revels in the full-blown privileges and joys of adult living.

---

[1] Matthew 25:14–30.

[2] *Answers.com/Wiki Answers.* (A New Testament talent was a measure of silver equal to approximately fifteen years' wages. Fifteen years times $15,000 equals $225,000.)

Discussion Ideas

- What are the advantages and disadvantages of allowing children to participate in the family's decision-making process?

- Under what circumstances should a parent allow a child to make a mistake?

- In the story of Adam and Eve, they acted irresponsibly, and God lost trust in them and reduced their freedom (Genesis 3:8–10). In explaining to your child how responsibility leads to trust, and trust leads to freedom, what are some examples you could give to your child?

- It is often difficult for us to allow our child to make a mistake in public without thinking that it reflects badly upon us. Share an example.

Chapter 16

When You Are Trying to Build Resilience...

Are they servants of Christ? (I am out of my mind to talk like this.) I am more. I have worked much harder, been in prison more frequently, been flogged more severely, and been exposed to death again and again. Five times I received from the Jews the forty lashes minus one. Three times I was beaten with rods, once I was stoned, three times I was shipwrecked, I spent a night and a day in the open sea, I have been constantly on the move. I have been in danger from rivers, in danger from bandits, in danger from my own countrymen, in danger from Gentiles; in danger in the city, in danger in the country, in danger at sea; and in danger from false brothers. I have labored and toiled and have often gone without sleep; I have known hunger and thirst and have often gone without food; I have been cold and naked. Besides everything else, I face daily the pressure of my concern for all the churches (2 Corinthians 11:23–28).

T he primary task of a parent is giving his or her child the gift of unconditional love. It is the key factor in allowing a child to experience high self-esteem and to value himself as a child of God. Unconditional love opens possibilities for quality, courageous living. It is also the key to resiliency.

By the way, when we use the term "resilience" in regard to our children, we are talking about enabling them to "keep on keeping on" in the face of adversity. While today's world offers unparalleled opportunities for exploration of possibilities and the actualization of potential, it can also be a dangerous playground for children and youth. Easy access to alcohol and drugs, the invitation to casual sex, and a culture that extols violence in film and art are among the clear and present dangers. Many times, the young person has experienced some kind of loss: a friend or loved one has died; a boyfriend or girlfriend has broken off a relationship; the family has recently moved to a new place of residence; or the young person has suffered a failure (or a fear of failure) that has resulted in feelings of diminished self-worth. Promoting resilience in our children allows them to transcend these and other traumas and perils of childhood and adolescence.

There is a parable on resiliency about a farmer who owned an old mule.

The mule fell into an old dry well on the farm. The farmer heard the mule braying and went out to find him. When he discovered the animal at the bottom of the well, he found himself in a dilemma. It would cost a lot of money to rent equipment to lift the mule out, and the farmer finally decided that neither the mule nor the well were worth the trouble of saving. So, he called his neighbors together, told them what had happened, and asked them to help him haul enough dirt to bury the old mule in the well and put him out of his misery. They dumped a big load of dirt alongside the well and began to shovel it into the hole.

At first, the old mule was hysterical. Then, as the farmer and his neighbors continued shoveling, and the dirt hit his back—a concept dawned in the mule's primitive mind. It suddenly struck him that every time a shovel of dirt hit his back, he could shake it off and step up. And this he did, shovelful after shovelful. "Shake it off, and step up…shake it off, and step up…shake it off, and step up…" was the mantra that filled his simple brain. No matter how painful the blows, or how distressing and hopeless the situation appeared to be, the old mule fought his panic and just kept right on, shaking it off and stepping up! He was saved by resilience.

And guess what? It was not very long before the old mule, battered and exhausted, stepped triumphantly over the wall of that well. What at first had seemed like a curse actually became his salvation…all because of the manner in which he handled his adversity. It is one of the key factors in building resilience. If we face our problems and respond to them positively instead of caving in to our feelings of panic, bitterness, and self-pity, we can usually transcend our difficulties and sometimes even turn them into blessings.

The key is our learning to "shake it off and step up" when the mud and dirt come flying our way.

One thing that can be a primary element in enabling children to "shake it off and step up" is consistently giving them encouragement. Everyone desperately needs the encouragement of the "significant others" in their lives. And, if we are the givers of that encouragement to the children in our midst, we quite literally become the "hands of the Christ"—dispensing the resiliency that will allow our child to endure and prevail.

A word of encouragement can take many forms. Sometimes it requires our being proactive—telling children that we appreciate who they are and what they do. Other times, it means being reactive— taking the time to *respond* when we see and hear kids crying out for help. It may be as simple as giving a pat on the back and saying the words, "I really appreciate how hard you are trying." It may mean telling a child who is experiencing a really tough time, "You are not going to have to go through this alone. I will be there for you all the way through!" Letting children know that we will always be there for them is a powerful encouragement for them to shake it off—whatever it is—and to step up.

If there was ever a person who knew what the bottom of a well looks like, it was the Apostle Paul. He was beaten, stoned, shipwrecked, and spent days adrift at sea. How did he make it through all those hardships without giving up? If you have read the book of

Acts, you may have noticed how Paul almost never traveled alone. He usually took someone with him on his missionary journeys. Paul's favorite traveling companion was a man called Barnabas. It was a nickname. Do you know what it meant? Acts 4:36 tells us, "There was a Levite, a native of Cyprus, Joseph, to whom the apostles gave the name Barnabas (which means 'son of encouragement')." The disciples would not have given Barnabas that nickname when they first met him. He would have become "Mr. Encouragement" only after they had seen him in action on his travels with Paul.

Paul could not have done many of the things he did—he would not have been able to suffer through all the hardships and persecutions and then to use those experiences in such a positive way—had it not been for the constant, unwavering encouragement of Barnabas. No wonder Paul insisted that the "son of encouragement" be his traveling companion. Paul ended up writing over half of the New Testament, and it probably would not have happened without Barnabas. May we parents be a Barnabas—a source of encouragement—to our child.

Sometimes, encouragement means just being there to listen to a child, to hold him, to weep with him, to be someone who is "safe" and who cares about him. We need to be on constant alert as to how we can be a source of encouragement to our child—giving him the strength and courage to persevere and not give up in spite of hardship and adversity.

Another way in which parents can help their child to become resilient is through the gift of perspective. Because of their limited experience, children tend to view minor personal setbacks or embarrassments as being far more catastrophic than they actually are.

A caring adult should first empathize and acknowledge to the child how difficult the particular setback or loss can feel. Then the adult can share that breaking up with a boyfriend, making a bad grade, losing a game, or getting bullied online is not "the end of the world" and that there is hope for the future. Most of the things that seem so painful and embarrassing at the time they occur are events of nonconcern to practically everyone else—and are usually soon forgotten. When parents share with a child some of their own stories of personal embarrassment—with a sense of humor if possible—it helps a child frame his perceived tragedy in a more positive light.

One of my own favorites, which my children found humorous when I shared it with them, occurred when I was in the ninth grade. I was on a student committee charged with picking out wristwatches for the "Most Outstanding" boy and girl at Bowie Junior High in Odessa, Texas. I was sitting on the front row in the auditorium in our closing school assembly when the winners were to be named. My delusions of personal grandeur were so great that when our principal said, "And the winner of the watch for the "Most Outstanding Boy" award is…" and then paused for dramatic emphasis, I actually rose to my feet to claim my watch—but had to sit back down again when the principal announced the name of someone else.

I lived through that embarrassment as well as many, many others. Our children will do the same, and part of our job as a parent is to convince them that the future holds great promise and that the tragedies of the moment will be of small consequence with the passage of time.

Jesus would take the gift of perspective a step further by telling His child that there are resurrection possibilities inherent in even the worst of personal tragedies. Michael Jordan was cut from his ninth grade basketball team. That personal failure prompted Michael to practice and train harder than everyone else around him, and he ended up becoming probably the best player to ever play the game. Jesus would tell his child, "Don't give up. The best of life is still yet to come."

Of course, Jesus' most powerful tool in building resilience in his child would be His gift of unconditional love. We can survive being rejected by almost everyone if just one person loves us "no matter what." Every child is entitled to that kind of love from a parent. It is the key to resiliency—the gift that enables a child to emerge from the emotional storms of adolescence and to enter adulthood emotionally and spiritually intact.

Dr. B. Glenn Wilkerson

Discussion Ideas

- Who was your greatest source of resilience when you were a child? How did he or she build your resiliency?

- Can you think of a personal story to share with your child regarding an embarrassing or painful event that you endured when you were growing up—something that seemed large to you when it occurred? How has the passage of time changed your perspective on the importance of that event?

- On a scale of 1–10, with 1 being "not very resilient" and 10 being "very resilient," how would you rate your child? How can you help build her resiliency?

- What do you see happening in your child's life that poses a challenge to his resiliency? What can you do to help ease that challenge?

PART V

Jesus' Approach to Some Difficult Issues

Chapter 17

Focusing Our Communication

With many similar parables Jesus spoke the word to them, as much as they could understand. He did not say anything to them without using a parable. But when He was alone with His own disciples, He explained everything (Mark 4:33–34).

"Attention deficit" is a modern term, but there is nothing new about the concept to which the term refers. Jesus was continuously frustrated by the short attention span and the seemingly deaf ears of His listeners.

A frequent complaint of parents is: "My child doesn't listen to me. Talking to her is like talking to a wall." Communicating well with our children is a common goal of every household, and it is frustrating when that communication breaks down or is ineffective.

Katrina, age eleven, was playing with friends a half block away from her home. Her mother wanted her to come home for dinner and called to her from the front door, "Katrina, come home. Dinner's ready." Katrina ignored her mother and kept on playing. Her mother called to her again, and Katrina kept on playing, acting as if she had not heard.

One of her playmates said, "Katrina, your mother is calling you home."

She replied, "I know. But she hasn't yelled yet!"

Katrina, like many children, had become "parent-deaf"—an affliction common to many homes.

Katrina's mother needs to confront the misbehavior of her daughter; and, to avoid more parent-deafness upon the part of Katrina, she can employ the technique of "focused communication." There are a variety of settings where focused communication is a valuable communication tool—especially when parents are instructing a child, reprimanding a child, or trying to reach a clear understanding with a child.

Most of the time, lengthy parent-child conversations are both appropriate and desirable. The rule of thumb for *focused* communication, however, is "the shorter, the better."

For example, in the case of family meetings, where rules, boundaries, and consequences are being negotiated, the most productive meetings will be those of thirty minutes or less. When a parent is confronting an individual child to correct a behavior or to impose a consequence, the more effective talks usually last no longer than five minutes. Longer lectures often give way to "issue-dumping," where the parent brings up every real and perceived problem that has occurred over a period of months. Once begun, an issue-dump usually deteriorates into an angry barrage of criticisms, damaging the self-esteem of the child and the child's relationship with the parent.

Effective communicators are aware of their audience's attention span. Most people can "hear" for fifteen to eighteen minutes if the talk is interesting, affirming, or humorous. However, when it comes to receiving criticism, even of a constructive nature, the average person has a three to five-minute attention span.

Here are some parental guidelines for engaging in focused communication with your child when confronting her misbehavior:

- Allow for a cooling-off period. If the child has behaved in a manner that angers you, take twenty minutes to "cool off" before talking with your child. Take a parent's time-out.
- Focus on the *specific* behavior you want to discuss with your child.
- Calmly remind the child of the logical consequences of that behavior.
- Stick to the point when discussing the behavior and the resulting age-appropriate consequences. End the discussion in five minutes or less (the five minute rule).

The South African Zulu tribe has developed an alternative to the five-minute rule. Each speaker is limited to what he can say while standing on one foot. As soon as the other foot touches the ground, that person must cease talking. It is an effective system for helping "wordy" talkers to maintain their focus while they are communicating.

Focused communication requires preparation—thinking about what to say and how to say it in a short period of time. When He was in a teaching mode, Jesus used storytelling to capture the short attention span of His listeners, He imparted profound thoughts by sharing brief, easy-to-remember stories. It is a tactic that Jesus would use with His child.

Also, focused communication is a two-way street. While it is a valuable tool in helping us to communicate our thoughts and feelings, it is equally useful in helping a child to express himself. This latter goal requires a technique of focused communication called *"active listening"* which means:

- Give the child good eye contact.
- Pay careful attention to the child's verbal and nonverbal messages.
- Repeat (or reflect) the child's message back to the child, and do so in a manner that indicates warmth and concern.

Parents who become skilled in the art of active listening will even rephrase the child's message as they repeat it back, using different words, thereby ensuring that the child really feels that she has been heard. For example, if the child says, "I hate going to the playground," a good active listener might reflect back, "You'd rather not go to the playground today?" Active listening helps the child to feel that he is truly being heard and encourages him to say more.

A wonderful example of active listening is Jesus' encounter with a Samaritan woman at the well outside of the city of Sychar. The woman told Jesus, "I have no husband." Jesus said to her, "You are right in saying, 'I have no husband'; for you have had five husbands, and the one you have now is not your husband. What you have said is true!" In reflecting her words back to her, Jesus listened to the woman with an intentness unlike anything she had ever experienced before.[1] In doing so, He made her feel valued.

Active listening is a marvelous tool in healing broken relationships. It can help relieve a child's negative feelings when we listen to her actively, quietly, and nonjudgmentally. Dorothy Briggs says in her book *Your Child's Self-Esteem*:

> The fastest way to get rid of negative emotions (and the only way to ensure that they won't erupt in unhealthy ways) is to encourage their expression. Negative feelings expressed and accepted lose their destructive power.[2]

Communication that heals and builds relationships begins with focused, active listening.

Focused communication (including active listening) is a learned skill that can make a huge difference in the quality of parent-child relationships. For example, Katrina's mother could sit down with her child, look her in the eye, and very quietly say, "Katrina, I know that you hear me calling you to come for dinner. From now on, if I call you, and you don't come to eat within five minutes, your dinner will be discarded, and you will have nothing to eat for the rest of the evening. Do we understand each other, honey? Do you have any questions?" By keeping the conversation to less than three minutes, using a calm warm voice, and employing a logical consequence in response to Katrina's misbehavior, the mother can use focused communication to help correct Katrina's "parent-deafness."

Because it is respectful and considerate of the attention span and the thoughts and feelings of others, focused communication is a form of unconditional love. Caring parents should follow the practices of Jesus in developing this skill for use with their children.

[1] John 4:17–19.

[2] Dorothy Corkville Briggs, *Your Child's Self-Esteem.* New York: Doubleday, 1975, p. 181.

- Have any of your children become "parent-deaf"? Share what you think would happen if you said to that child, "There is something I'd like to discuss with you. Let's keep the discussion to just five minutes. Then, if we want to, we can talk more about it later."

- What typically happens when you go "on and on" when discussing a violation of a rule and the resulting consequence with your child?

- Were your parents skilled at communicating with you? Do you communicate differently with your child? If so, how?

- Jesus actively listened to the woman at the well and made her feel like a valued child of God. How does it make you feel when someone "actively listens" to you? Do you regularly—and intentionally—actively listen to your child?

Chapter 18
Bully-Proofing

The Philistines stood on the mountain on the one side, and Israel stood on the mountain on the other side, with a valley between them....The Philistine giant, Goliath, said, "Today I defy the ranks of Israel! Give me a man, that we may fight together....When Saul and all Israel heard these words of the Philistine, they were dismayed and greatly afraid.... David said to Saul, "Let no one's heart fail because of Goliath; your servant will go and fight with this Philistine [bully]...."

David ran quickly toward the battle line to meet the Philistine. David put his hand in his bag, took out a stone, slung it, and struck the Philistine on his forehead; the stone sank into his forehead, and Goliath fell face down on the ground. So David prevailed over the Philistine with a sling and a stone, striking down the Philistine and killing him (1 Samuel 17:3, 10–11, 32, 48–50).

I n our current culture, bullying is epidemic, and its impact upon kids is tragic. One-third of teens report being bullied.[1] Every day, 160,000 kids miss school for fear of being bullied.[2] Parents need to provide bully-proofing skills to protect their children against the physical, verbal, and emotional abuse common among youth today.

Traditional Bullying

The type of bullying that most of today's adults knew when they were kids is now called "traditional bullying." There are several kinds of traditional bullies: physical bullies, verbal bullies, and social bullies.

Physical bullies push, hit, and kick their victim and steal or damage their victim's property. Verbal bullies use words to injure their victim with humiliation by calling names, throwing out insults, or making racist or sexist comments. Still another type is a social bully. Social bullies try to convince others to exclude or reject someone. They cut the victims off from their social connections. These bullies (usually girls) do this through gossip or by spreading rumors. Bullying may take on any of these forms, but it has the same devastating effect.

Goliath is a classic example of a physical bully. A giant of a man, he intimidated and bullied the entire army of Israel. When David ran out to meet him, Goliath thought that the teenage boy would be an easy victim. To everyone's amazement, David not only confronted his tormenter—he defeated him! However, while David's use of force in defeating Goliath makes for a thrilling story, it is too dangerous an option for kids to use in confronting physical bullies today.

Giving children the tools to cope with "physical bullying" can be an important element in the development and strength of their self-esteem. Adults should encourage children to show a confident, assertive attitude when dealing with bullies. Instruct your child, "Even if you have to fake it, act strong because bullies pick on kids whom they think are weak."

Here are some things to tell your kids in helping them to deal with physical bullies:

- If you are being bullied, try to avoid being caught alone. Stick close to friends or classmates.
- If a bully confronts you, walk away from the bully and ignore him. If the bully does not get a reaction out of you, he might get bored with trying.
- Walk tall with your head held high and look the bully in the eye. Smile at the bully. Try to think up funny responses ahead of time and use them to surprise the bully. A quick and witty response is not what he is hoping for.
- Be sure to use a strong, assertive voice without a hint of whining. Using your "strong voice," tell the bully, "Leave me alone!"

- If you feel that you or another person might be in physical danger, tell an adult. Share your problem with a parent, another family member, or maybe a teacher or counselor. If you find it hard to discuss, write it down and give it to an adult you trust.[3]

It is important for children to understand that the same techniques used in confronting youthful bullies are to be used in confronting adult bullies as well. Sometimes children feel it is rude or wrong to challenge the behavior of adults who inflict abusive behavior upon them. Our children should be given permission and encouragement to confront anyone—young or old—who assaults their worth or tries to get them to engage in behavior that "feels wrong" to them. And, if they have been mistreated by an adult bully (or abuser), our children need to know that they *must* tell another caring adult.

If you become aware that your child is being bullied at school or in the neighborhood, keep a written record of the incidents, including the names of the children involved, the date, what happened, and where it took place. Meet with your child's teacher and share your concerns in a friendly, non-confrontational way. Ask the teacher how well your child seems to be getting along with others. Has she ever noticed your child being excluded or isolated by other children? Also, ask the teacher to investigate and to take action to help stop the bullying. Then schedule a follow-up conference with the teacher to discuss any actions that have been taken.

If you are concerned with how well your child is handling the stress of being bullied, ask to see the school's guidance counselor. If the situation persists, talk with the school principal. Be sure to keep notes on your meetings with the teacher and school officials.

Cyber-bullying

A new type of bullying that kids are experiencing today is called "cyber-bullying." Cyber-bullies use electronic technology, such as computers and cell phones, to harass or embarrass other kids. It employs text messaging, sexting, instant messages, identity and password theft, and e-mails to humiliate and embarrass the targeted person. It can be even more hurtful and long-lasting than traditional bullying, because it can be sent to a wide audience, and it follows the victim anywhere they use their cell phone or log on to the Internet. Because the bully can make up an identity or steal one from someone else, the messages often are anonymous, and the victim does not know who the bully is.

Cyber-bullying might come in the form of an anonymous Internet message to your child:

I hate you.
Everybody else hates you, too.
You should just die!

Or your child might be targeted on a "bashing" Web site where other kids vote on the fattest, ugliest, and most unpopular kid at school:

See pictures of the five ugliest fat kids
at Tremont Intermediate School.
Vote for the ugliest, fattest kid by clicking here.

Cyber-bullying campaigns are usually not successful without the help, intended or not, of other children. And, if given an anonymous method of reporting cyber-bullying campaigns and Web sites, kids can put an end to it. Parents should make sure that school officials and community groups provide a way (usually a Web site) for children to easily and anonymously report bullying.

We must teach our children that remaining silent when another person is being hurt is not acceptable, and that they must take action to prevent cyber-cruelty from taking place. As Martin Luther King Jr. said, "In the end, we will remember not the words of our enemies, but the silence of our friends."

To prevent cyber-bullying, use your "parental control" options. Talk with your child regularly about the Internet activities in which he is involved. Tell your child that you will keep tabs on her online account if you think there is a reason for concern. Inform her that while you respect her privacy, her safety is even more important to you. Tell your child that hurting others is unacceptable and harmful and that there will be consequences if he participates in any inappropriate online behavior. Also, instruct your child to never share his password with anybody other than you.

It is important to encourage your child to tell you immediately if she is being cyber-bullied. Assure her that you will not confiscate her technology if she confides in you. If you discover that your child is being cyber-bullied, there are several things you should do:

- Discourage your child from responding to the cyber-bullying.
- Instruct your child to block communication with the cyber-bully and to not pass along any cyber-bullying messages.
- Tell your child to share the words or pictures with you (so you can save them as evidence) and then to remove the painful message(s) from his computer.
- Try to identify the person doing the cyber-bullying.
- If the cyber-bullying is taking place through the school's Internet system, the school has an obligation to prevent it. Contact the school for help.
- Consider contacting the cyber-bully's parents. If you do decide to contact them, do so in writing or over the phone—not in person. Present evidence of the cyber-bullying (for example, copies of e-mail messages) and ask them to put a stop to the cyber-bullying.

- Contact the police—and possibly involve an attorney—if the cyber-bullying contains items such as threats of violence, child pornography, sexual exploitation, or a picture of someone taken in a place where she would expect privacy.[4]

It is important to not be a passive bystander if your child is being cyber-bullied. Get involved in stopping it.

Preventing Your Child from Becoming a Bully

Bullying is damaging to the lives of both the victim and the bully. Dr. Duane Alexander, director of the National Institute of Child Health and Development, says, "People who were bullied as children are more likely to suffer from depression and low self-esteem well into adulthood, and the bullies themselves are more likely to engage in criminal behavior later in life."[5]

Bullies suffer from low self-esteem. Because of their insecurities, they try to "put down" other people in order to feel dominant and powerful. Often, they act the way they do because they themselves have been hurt by bullies in the past—maybe by a parent or some other family member.

Parents can help their children to avoid being bullies by enabling them to experience feelings of being competent and powerful in positive and constructive ways, and providing them the unconditional love that builds self-esteem—thereby reducing their need to build themselves up by putting down those around them.

Preventing Your Child from Being Victimized by a Bully

The human community itself has a responsibility to see that our children are not bullied. An article, coauthored by former U.S. Department of Health and Human Services Secretary Kathleen Sebelius and U.S. Department of Education Secretary Arne Duncan, says that the most promising approaches to combating bullying are those that "get entire communities involved. When principals, teachers, school nurses, pediatricians, social workers, faith leaders, law enforcement agents, parents and youth all have the information they need to recognize bullying and respond to it, bullies get a clear message that their behavior is unacceptable."[6] Many schools are now addressing the need for a campus-wide anti-bullying program. If your child is experiencing problems with a bully, talk to the school about implementing an anti-bullying program on the campus. Most bullies "play to the crowd," and, if the crowd has the courage and compassion to say, "Stop that!" "That's not funny!" "That's cruel!" the bullying will end.

The most valuable role that a parent can play in "bully-proofing" a child is to extend the unconditional love that allows a child to continue to value himself in spite of the hurtful words and actions of others. Armed with the sure knowledge that he is valued and loved—

no matter what!—a child can acquire the skills that prevent him from being emotionally traumatized by the verbal taunts, physical intimidation, and cyber-cruelty of bullies.

While Jesus and His contemporaries did not have to deal with the current cyber-bullying phenomena, other forms of bullying were as rampant in His time as they are in ours. He verbally confronted the religious bullies who put other people down and ridiculed their beliefs. In like fashion, Jesus would not stand idly by and allow His child to be bullied. He would do all within His power to make sure that His child was protected from any verbal, emotional, or physical cruelty that could undermine His child's innate feelings of worth.

[1] "Mothering," May/June 2001.

[2] National Center for Educational Statistics and Bureau of Justice Statistics, "Indicators of School Crime and Safety: 2009 [online]

[3] Karen L. Swan, *ARK for Teens Manual*, pp. 24–25.

[4] Robert Garofalo et. al., "Archives of Pediatric and Adolescent Medicine, May 1999, 153:487 ff.

[5] Duane Alexander, "Survey Finds Bullying Widespread in U.S. Schools," National Institute of Child Health and Human Development, NIH News Release, April 24, 2001. http://www.nichd.nih.gov

[6] Kathleen Sebelius and Arne Duncan, "We must protect kids from bullying," Op/Ed article in *Houston Chronicle/San Diego Union Tribune/St. Paul Pioneer Press*, October 9, 2010. http://www.chron.com/disp/story.mpl/editorial/outlook/7239697.html

Discussion Ideas

- David defeated Goliath by force. That is not an option today. What tactics can a parent teach a child to prevent him from being victimized by a physical bully?
- What are some things you can do to prevent your child from bullying others?
- What advice can you give to your child if she becomes the victim of a cyber-bully?
- How do you think you and other parents can work with your child's teachers and her school to prevent bullying?

Chapter 19
Coaching Emotional Control

Parents, do not treat your children in such a way as to make them angry. Instead, bring them up with Christian discipline and instruction (Ephesians 6:4).

A study conducted at the University of Washington in Seattle shows that the way parents deal with both their own emotions and their children's emotions may have a major effect on their children's physical health, academic achievement, and emotional well-being. The study suggests that, as parents teach their children how to understand and manage their emotions, the children experience less stress and are able to focus better in school. As a result, the children have longer attention spans and are able to score higher on math and achievement tests. The children of emotionally-skilled parents also appear to have less behavioral problems in school, at home, and with their friends.[1]

The way people experience and express their emotions depends, in part, on heredity. Some people are born with the ability to openly express their emotions while others keep their feelings to themselves. However, regardless of their genetics, children can be "coached" on handling their feelings. Loving parents who are willing to expend the time, patience, and energy on teaching their children to be aware of their emotions—and to express those emotions in acceptable ways—provide a great gift that will bless their children throughout their lives.

Emotional coaching begins with creating a loving and accepting atmosphere for discussing feelings with our children. We can tell children that, while feelings can be expressed in positive or negative ways, feelings themselves are neither good nor bad; they just *are*. Instead of feeling guilty over feelings of resentment and anger, children can be encouraged to talk about their feelings and to discover acceptable ways of expressing them. We do children a disservice by teaching them to deny their feelings. Repressed emotions do not go away; they will resurface later, and often in a more explosive manner. On the other hand, feelings that are acknowledged and accepted tend to lose their destructive power over us.

So, the first step in helping children to handle their emotions is to teach them to examine their feelings rather than denying or repressing them. We inhibit a child's ability to manage her feelings when we react to the child's feelings with a lecture or a reprimand or by ridiculing the child and making her feel guilty. Instead of telling a child she should not feel a certain way, we can simply reflect the feeling back to the child, using language that helps the child to understand the feeling and to explore it further. In the process, we can give the child some vocabulary for an appropriate expression of her feelings. For example, rather than saying to her, "Don't say you hate your brother. You shouldn't feel that way!" we can say, "You sound like you are really angry with your brother right now," or "I don't like your using that language. Can you tell me what you are feeling?" Through "active listening" (see page 182), we can encourage the child to talk about the feeling and to explore her options for dealing with it in a positive manner.

We must explain to our children how important it is that they learn to exercise some control over their emotions. When they learn the techniques of emotional control, they will perform better, behave better, and be far more successful in every aspect of life. (Some of the anger-management techniques that adults can use in controlling their emotions—discussed in Chapter 13—can be equally helpful with children.) We can teach a child that—if he is feeling anxious or uptight—there are four simple things he can do to relieve the pressure:

- "Take deep breaths." (Even one deep breath provides extra oxygen and relaxes the muscles associated with the breathing process. The result is an almost immediate reduction in mental and physical tension.)

- "Do physical exercise." (A fast-paced walk, playing basketball, jumping rope, or a workout at the gym produces endorphins, the body chemical that reduces stress.)

- "Take a time-out." (If a child feels like he is about to explode with frustration or anger, a five-minute time-out can help him to calm his emotions so that he can respond to the situation in a rational manner.)

- "Talk to someone you trust who will listen without judgment." (Talking to a parent, teacher, counselor, or clergyperson can help the child to understand the feeling, and, in the process, vent and release it.)

Special attention needs to be given to children who are dealing with "troubling" feelings such as fear and anger. We should give kids tools for expressing these feelings appropriately, so that they do not hurt themselves or others. For example, we can tell children that physical exercise and "talking about their feelings with someone who cares" are good ways to release feelings of anger. We can even provide a "punching pillow" to help them vent their anger, or we can accompany our children on a brisk walk while they talk through their feelings.

When confronted by a child's anger or fear, it is always appropriate to ask ourselves, "What is the unmet need of this child?

How can I help meet her unmet need?" or, "What is he afraid of? How can I assist him in confronting his fears?"

We can also coach a child to become emotionally skilled—in terms of dealing with troubling feelings—by asking questions that will help the child to analyze and to solve the problem causing the feeling. Instead of saying, "A big boy like you shouldn't be afraid of the dark," we can say, "What do you think can be done to make your room less scary at night?" It is important to help children see that they have a responsibility for choosing their behavior. As we encourage our children to examine their feelings and to explore acceptable ways of resolving them, we create in them the confidence that they can handle their emotions and solve their own problems. Providing that confidence is a primary function of a loving, nurturing parent.

In helping children to manage their feelings, parents should be aware of the tone of voice and the communication style they use when discussing a child's misbehavior. It is helpful to use "I-messages" rather than "U-messages" when describing the problem. For example, we can say, "I am upset that you didn't do your homework at the time you were supposed to do it," rather than, "You made me angry because you didn't do your homework on time." U-messages put the child on the defensive. I-messages, on the other hand, make it much easier for the child to "hear" the complaint without getting angry or defensive.

We must not only learn how to handle our own feelings, but also to teach our children how to handle theirs. Thinking that they have no options, many young people allow themselves to be slaves to their emotions. They say, "That's just the way I am. I have a hot temper." Unfortunately, emotionally immature people never grow up. They function as children all of their lives. A primary goal in parenting is to enable our children to mature as emotionally responsible persons. We can promote their growth by coaching them in how to deal with their feelings in positive ways.

When Jesus was confronted by His enemies in the Garden of Gethsemane, His disciple Peter became enraged. He drew his sword and cut off one of the soldier's ears. Jesus admonished Peter to control his emotions.[2] He would similarly instruct His child.

[1]   *Houston Chronicle*, June 3, 1994, pp. 1E, 8E.
[2]   John 18:10–11.

Discussion Ideas

- Describe why you think it is important to let your children know that "while feelings can be expressed in positive or negative ways, feelings are neither good nor bad. They just *are*."

- Whenever Jesus was feeling anxious, He would go to the mountains for a personal retreat (sometimes for just a day) to sort out His thoughts and feelings. Then He would come back and be a source of comfort and peace to those around Him (Matthew 14:23; Luke 6:23). When you feel angry or anxious, how do you go about calming your spirit so that you can model emotional control to your children?

- Some children are genetically "hardwired" to express their emotions openly. Other children are more reserved in showing how they feel. How about your child?

- Give an illustration of how you might guide your child to express his feelings in an appropriate manner.

Chapter 20

Letting Go

Train a child in the way he should go, and when he is old he will not turn from it (Proverbs 22:6).

There is a passage that older teens go through called "declaring of personhood." While a number of books about the teenage years have described this passage of life, most parents still think the problems they are encountering are unique to their family.

A young person's "declaring of personhood" is not something that a child is consciously aware of doing. However, it is a developmental stage of a teenager's life that is as natural and normal as puberty. It consists of a young person going through a time when he will reject the value system of his parents and embrace instead the value system of his peer group. It is a necessary part of the maturing process, and those who do not participate in it do not grow up. At age thirty, they will still be "momma's boys" and "daddy's girls" and living at home. (And who wants that?)

Author and friend John Bradshaw says that when it comes time for a teen to declare his personhood, and there is not really an issue between him and his parents for him to rebel against, he will create one. It is something he has to do to declare his personhood.[1]

This stage usually lasts anywhere from six months to five years, and it almost always results in the young person coming back into relationship with his parents and adopting the parental values against which he rebelled. The new relationship, however, will be different from what existed before. Prior to the passage, the child will have had a dependent relationship with his parents. After establishing his personhood, he will begin relating to his mother and father both as peers and as parents. The resulting relationship should be the ultimate goal of every adult who is involved in the process of parenting.

The passage varies greatly from person to person, depending upon their emotional makeup and level of self-esteem. Kids with high self-esteem will usually demonstrate their rejection of parental values in relatively innocuous ways—such as choice of friends, music, dress, and hairstyles. Those with low self-esteem will generally "act out" their feelings in a more radical manner. Their declaration may include defying authority, dropping out of school, and heavy experimentation with alcohol, drugs, and sex.

One family had two daughters, ages fourteen and sixteen, who were beautiful and popular but had very low self-esteem. The sixteen-year-old ran away from home with her twenty-one-year-old boyfriend, and, two weeks later, the fourteen-year-old ran away with her eighteen-year-old boyfriend. Both girls dropped out of school, and, for six months, were heavily involved in drugs and alcohol. That was thirty years ago. Those two girls have now matured into adults with families of their own and are highly regarded and respected women. Because of their low self-esteem, they declared their personhood in a radical fashion. However, upon completion of their passage, both girls essentially came back to embrace the values of their parents.

To become an independent adult, every adolescent must navigate through this passage. What is different about kids declaring their personhood today is that they are doing so at a much earlier age than their parents did. Most adults who are now in their thirties and forties (and older) went through this passage after age eighteen when they had graduated from high school and moved on either to college or to take a job. Such is not the case with today's youth. They are maturing at an earlier age. So, their temporary rejection of their parent's values usually takes place while they are still living at home, with the result that parents today find themselves in conflict with their thirteen to eighteen-year-old children without either party really understanding why.

Since little information about this passage of life has been shared, most parents think the difficulties they are encountering are unique to their family. Not true! While the degree of the behavior will vary from child to child, virtually all kids go through this passage.

There are a number of things that parents can do that will help them and their children to more easily pass through this period of transition. First of all, it is important to realize that most families with teenage youth are experiencing this same situation. It is a normal life-passage, and, as with all passages, one day it will end. Parents can take comfort in the knowledge that there is "light at the end of the tunnel."

Secondly, it is critical that parents retain their value system. Instead of "giving in" to adolescent standards of behavior, adults should offer their kids a strong set of values against which they can rebel and to which they can later return. One parent related that he had caught his teenage son smoking pot with his friends. After talking it over with him, they struck a deal. The father would allow the boy to smoke pot in his room if he would not smoke it on the streets with his friends. That is crazy parenting. Now the boy has to pick out some other parental value to rebel against. Parents must not compromise their value system. Kids need some core values to rebel against and to which they can return after the passage is over.

Thirdly, parents can help facilitate this process by allowing an older child greater participation in the making of family decisions that directly affect her. As children sense the respect of adults, they will no longer feel as great a need to declare their personhood in inappropriate ways.

Finally, and most importantly, *adults can let their children know that they love them even though they disapprove of (and must discipline) their bad behavior.* Kids need to know that the key is always hanging on the outside of the door. And when a child is ready to come back into relationship with his parents, all he has to do is put the key in the lock, open the door, and walk back into the relationship.

Jesus' story of the Prodigal Son,[2] discussed in Chapter 1, reminds us that teenage rebellion against the parental value system should not be construed as a personal attack. It is a normal, appropriate passage in an adolescent's journey toward maturity. The father in Jesus' story did not disown his son, nor did he seek to punish his prodigal boy for his seeming ingratitude. He simply allowed the process to take place. Then, when the boy finished the passage and was ready to return home, his father ran to meet him. What a marvelous parental model for parents to follow in enabling our young people to declare their personhood.

The four points to remember in letting go and helping your child through the process of declaring personhood are:

- Recognize that it is a natural, normal, and appropriate stage in the child's development.
- Retain your parental value system so your teen will have values against which to rebel and later to return.
- As an older adolescent shows responsibility, give her more freedom to make decisions.

- Let your child know that you unconditionally love him
  even though you disapprove of, and must discipline, his
  inappropriate behavior.

The more we affirm our child's value and worth, the higher her self-esteem will be and the less she will feel compelled to act out her feelings while declaring her personhood. The good news, parents, is that "This, too, shall pass!" And the young person who comes back into relationship with you will be the independent, responsible, loving adult you have raised him to be.

Jesus would recognize His child's passage into adulthood as something both necessary and good. When it came time to do so, He would "let go," pray for His child's safe journey, and celebrate his return as an esteemed, lovable, forgiven child of God.

[1] John Bradshaw, "The Stages of Life," Lecture at Cypress Creek Christian Community Center, October 2004.
[2] Luke 15:11–24.

Discussion Ideas

- What was declaring your personhood like for you?

- How old were you when you entered this developmental passage? How long did it last?

- After declaring your personhood, did you come back to embrace most of your parent's core values as an adult? Give an example.

- While the boy in Jesus' story of the Prodigal Son was declaring his personhood, his father continued to extend unconditional love. What role do you think the father's love played in his son's development after the boy returned home?

Conclusion

Then Jesus took a little child and set him in the midst of them. And when He had taken him in His arms, He said to them, "Whoever receives one of these little children in My name receives Me; and whoever receives Me, receives not Me but Him who sent Me (Mark 9:36–37).

The primary element in a faith journey is God's unconditional love. It transforms and enriches lives—more so than anything else known to humankind. If Jesus had a child, He would take His child on that journey.

The First Pillar of Great Parenting

Jesus' first pillar of great parenting would be the giving and receiving of unconditional love. When intentionally shared with children, it becomes the building block of great family dynamics, blessing the parents as well as the kids.

Phil Mickelson is considered to be one of the best golfers ever to play the game. He is known for his brilliant shot-making and also for his taking risks in trying very difficult shots instead of "playing it safe." Sometimes those risky shots toward the end of a golf tournament enable him to be the winner. Other times, those risks cost him the tournament. One such case was the 2006 U.S. Open played at Winged Foot.

Phil stood on the tee box at the final hole of the tournament holding a one-shot lead. All he needed was to par the hole to win. He proceeded to hit a series of terrible shots and finished with a double bogey, losing one of the most prestigious tournaments in professional golf by one stroke. It was a staggering loss for Mickelson. He had practiced for months in hopes of winning this particular event.

Later that day, Phil was snuggling with his daughter Amanda, and she asked, "Are you okay, Dad?"

He replied, "Well, I'm a little disappointed. This was a tournament I dreamed of winning as a kid, and I haven't yet."

His daughter said, "Well, second is pretty good, Dad. Can I get you a piece of pizza?"

Reflecting back on that moment, Mickelson says, "It was kind of a bigger-picture perspective."

Two days later, Phil took his family to Disneyland, where he would be the focus of attention of tens of thousands of people, many of whom would be aware that he had just "blown" a major golf tournament. Mickelson's mind-set was, "It's time to move on. I know my wife loves me. I know my kids love me. I can't wait to tee it up next time."

Phil says, "My family has reduced the effect of my career on my self-esteem. When I'm with them, they make me feel special regardless of how I play."[1]

Since that tournament, Phil has proceeded to win many additional events, including the most prestigious of the four major tournaments, the Masters. That is the power of unconditional love! It is the key to resilience and high self-esteem. It is also the primary ingredient in personal spiritual growth.

Just as the unwavering love of his family empowered Phil Mickelson to live fully and courageously, Jesus would teach His child to live fully and courageously by informing her that God unconditionally loves her. It is Jesus' first pillar of great parenting: providing the unconditional love that allows a child to embrace her worth as a child of God.

The Second Pillar of Great Parenting

Jesus' second pillar of great parenting would be to instill a servant's heart in His child—the sort of heart modeled by a man named Bob Butler.

Bob Butler lost both of his legs in a 1965 land mine explosion in Vietnam. Twenty years later, he was working in his garage in a small town in Arizona on a hot summer day when he heard a woman's screams coming from the pool area in the backyard of a neighboring house. He started rolling his wheelchair toward the house, but the dense shrubbery would not allow him access to the backyard. So he got out of his chair and began to crawl through the dirt and bushes.

When Butler arrived at the pool, he found a three-year-old named Stephanie Hanes lying at the bottom. The little girl had been born without arms and had fallen in the water and could not swim. Her mother stood by the water, paralyzed with fear, screaming frantically. Butler dove to the bottom of the pool and brought the girl up to the surface and placed her on the pool deck. Stephanie's face was blue. She had no pulse and was not breathing. Butler immediately went to work performing CPR on the girl while Stephanie's mother called the fire department. Told that the paramedics were already out on another call, the mother sobbed and hugged Butler's shoulder. As Butler continued with his CPR, he tried to reassure her.

"Don't worry," he said between breaths. "I was her arms to get out of the pool. It'll be okay. I am now her lungs. Together we can make it."

A few seconds later, the little girl coughed, regained consciousness, and began to cry. As they hugged and rejoiced together, the mother asked Butler how he knew it would be okay.

"The truth is I didn't know," he said. "But when my legs were blown off in the war, I was all alone in a field. No one was there to help, except a little Vietnamese girl. As she struggled to drag me into her village, she whispered in broken English, 'It okay. You can live. I be your legs. Together we make it.'"[2]

"Together we make it." Those words are the rallying cry of a servant's heart. If Jesus were physically present today, He would surely be calling for a united global effort to eradicate hunger and preventable disease among the children of this world. And Jesus would not only raise His voice, He would model for His child a spiritual life where love is revealed through actions.

Jesus would take His child to homeless shelters and other venues where they could serve together in helping others. He would march on behalf of hungry kids and be a person to whom troubled teens could come and talk. He would write His political representatives, asking them to champion the cause of poor, uninsured children locally and across the nation. Jesus would take His child with Him as He went about sharing God's unconditional love, and He would say, "We must do what we can to make life better for others. Together, my child, we make it."

The Third Pillar of Great Parenting

Jesus' third pillar of great parenting would be for each of us to liberate ourselves from the unconscious repetition of parenting patterns that have been passed from generation to generation within our family.

This means consciously recognizing and embracing those behaviors that involve unconditionally loving and encouraging your child. It also requires intentionally discarding any parenting behaviors that are demeaning or abusive and that, in effect, have constituted a "family curse."

Do you remember growing up and saying to yourself, "I will *never* say the things to my child that my mother says to me," and "I will *never* beat my kids like my daddy did me!" Then we become parents, and we unconsciously repeat the same parenting behaviors that have been in place in our families for generations.

Following my sophomore year at the University of Texas, I came back home that summer to work. One afternoon, I saw a pickup truck next to mine—everybody drives pickups in Odessa, Texas!—and on that pickup was a bumper sticker that said, "My day ain't complete until I've caught hell from somebody!" I guess that slogan must have gotten imprinted on my subconscious, and, almost immediately, I got a chance to use it.

That very night, I slipped into our house an hour past my curfew. Next morning, I came into the kitchen to eat breakfast, and there sat my father at the kitchen table. Dad was a big man—6'3", 245 pounds, and a former professional football player. He said, "Son, why did you come home an hour late last night?"

Without thinking, I blurted out, "Well, all I know is, my day ain't complete until I've caught hell from somebody!"

He said, "What did you say?"

And I repeated it, "I *said* that my day ain't complete until I've caught hell from somebody!"

You would not believe a man that big could move that fast! In a heartbeat, he was out of his chair, and he was on me. He grabbed my arm, and I started running in a circle—with him as the pivot point. He did not actually want to hurt me. So, instead of using the toe of his shoe, he used the instep and started applying his foot to my behind as we spun around in a circle, with him yelling, "I'm your father! Show me some respect! Don't you ever talk to me that way again!"

That parenting behavior became seared into my unconscious memory. And, without the help of a friend, book, or program to help me challenge questionable parenting practices that had been passed down in my family, it was almost certain that I would repeat that behavior with my son, Kevin.

I got my chance when Kevin was in the eighth grade. We pulled into the driveway at our house one Saturday afternoon. And, as we got out of the car, I asked him to do something, and he said, "Make me!"

Without consciously thinking about what I was doing, I spun him around, grabbed him by the collar, and propelled him across the front lawn—just as my father had done, applying the instep of my shoe to his behind and yelling, "I'm your father! Show some respect for me! Don't you ever talk to me that way again!" To Kevin's absolute delight, we got halfway across the yard; and, out of the corner of my eye, I saw four cars that had stopped to watch the preacher abuse his kid.

The next morning, I had an early breakfast with a friend and told him what I had done. I said, "You know, I didn't abuse Kevin physically so much as I abused him emotionally. I shamed him in front of our entire neighborhood."

My friend said, "Glenn, where did that come from?"

And it instantly dawned on me. "My father did the same thing to me twenty-five years ago."

Questionable parenting behaviors are passed on from our parents to us and through us to our children, unless we consciously step back and analyze those behaviors and decide upon new and more appropriate ways of relating to our children.

Jesus' third pillar of great parenting entails having the insight and courage to liberate ourselves from the past. It requires our stepping back and taking an objective look at the parenting behaviors that have been passed down in our families for generations. Those parenting practices that were positive and revealed unconditional love will be passed on to our children, and those parenting techniques that demeaned us or conveyed conditional approval will be discarded. Then, with the help of the teachings of Jesus, we can employ a new parenting style that allows our child to feel embraced by the unconditional love of God.

Jesus' Ultimate Parenting Goal

The physical, mental, and emotional health of a child is important. However, if a child is to have a meaningful, joy-filled life, spiritual growth is essential. In fact, I believe it to be the most important element in a child's development. If things are not right spiritually—if a child's values and his sense of being valued are not intact—he will tend to squander his physical, mental, and emotional gifts.

Jesus would emphasize the spiritual. He would take His child on a journey of faith that highlights God's unconditional love and that inspires a servant's heart. Along the way, He would teach His child to laugh and to be grateful. That is what He would do…if Jesus had a child.

[1]   Kate Meyers, *Parade Magazine*, March 27, 2011.
[2]   Jack Canfield, Amy Seeger, and Barbara Russell Chesser, *Chicken Soup for the Golden Soul*, 2000, pp. 89–90.

Jesus' "Great Parenting" Checklist

Unconditional love means that we separate the person from the behavior and love a child for who he *is* rather than for what he *does*. Children who receive unconditional love develop high self-esteem and are enabled to value themselves as a child of God. If Jesus were to prepare a parenting checklist, it could look like this:

The Daily Checklist for Great Parenting:

1. Tell my child at least once a day, "I love you."
2. Give at least ten minutes of undivided attention to my child each day.
3. Look at my child when I listen and talk with her.
4. Touch my child in an appropriate, caring manner. (Hugs, kisses, arm around the shoulders, pats on the back, and holding hands can be important ways of showing a child that he is loved.)
5. Empathize with my child. Listen to her feelings without criticism.
6. Pray *for* my child—and *with* my child—every day.

Other Things to Remember:

1. Teach my child that God and Jesus love her.
2. Facilitate my child's spiritual growth by taking him to church.
3. Attend my child's activities.
4. Encourage the efforts of my child.
5. Use a "parent's time-out" to avoid touching my child when angry.
6. Establish reasonable boundaries for my child. (Children need a few basic rules for acceptable behavior and age-appropriate consequences that are consistently enforced when they break those rules.)

EPILOGUE

A Parent's Greatest Gift

The power of unconditional love in the life of a young person is incredible. My wife Karen and I had five children. Let me tell you about my oldest, a young man named Kevin.

He has always been an absolute joy to us. And, at the same time, Kevin was one of those kids who can present some real challenges to first-time parents.

Kevin has one of the highest intellects of anyone I know. (He takes after his mother.) You would think a kid like that would do great in school. Well, that was not the case. When he was growing up, he was a little bit hyperactive and a whole lot attention-deficit. He never did anything bad, but he was constantly in trouble at school for talking in class and playing the role of the class clown. Combine all that with being a preacher's kid, and you have a pretty active mix. I did not realize the extent of it until he started the first grade.

After the first six weeks, the first-grade classes at Kevin's school had an open house event. When we walked into Kevin's class, all the little desks were lined up in rows facing the teacher's desk, which was at the front of the classroom. All the desks, that is, except one. One little desk was lined up beside the teacher's desk, facing the rest of the classroom.

I asked Kevin, "Where's your desk?"

He said, "That's mine up at the front with the teacher's desk."

We pulled the teacher aside and asked her why Kevin's desk was next to hers. She said, "He talks all the time. I can't keep his attention. I'm five minutes into a lesson, and he's lost interest and is talking to the kids around him. And, if I ask a rhetorical question, he blurts out the answer. Finally, in order to keep him from talking to the other students, I moved his desk up here next to mine. And now he spends all day talking to me!"

As we were leaving open house that evening, we drove through the parking lot past the school's main entrance. An impressive-looking man, dressed in a tie and a three-piece suit, was standing on the curb, waving to the cars as they passed by. When our car got directly across from the man, Kevin rolled down his window and leaned out and shouted, "Daryl! Daryl! How are you?"

The man waved and said, "Kevin Wilkerson! I'll see you tomorrow!"

I asked Kevin, "Who was that?"

He said, "Oh, that's Daryl Ludiker, my principal. I go see him every day."

I ended up being on a first-name basis with every teacher, counselor, and principal that boy had in twelve years of school.

We made it through twelve years of school, and Kevin ended up getting a soccer scholarship at Clemson University. That summer, before he was to leave for his freshman year in college, was a difficult one for our family. He was declaring his personhood and testing his parents one last time before leaving the nest. Two times during the summer, I came home and found Karen in tears over something Kevin had done. On both occasions, I listened and became furious with him. The second time, I told Karen, "I don't care if I am a preacher. As soon as that boy gets home, I'm going to take him out in the backyard and beat the 'H' out of him!"

Karen looked startled and then began to laugh. She said, "Go to our bathroom and look at your "Daily Checklist" you've got taped to the mirror. You know that you promised to never touch our children when you are angry." Her laughter and the "Daily Checklist" served to calm my anger, and the moment passed. But let me tell you…it was a tumultuous three months.

Late August finally came, and we loaded everyone in the van and headed for Clemson, South Carolina. Our family is really affectionate with one another. And, since Kevin would be the first child to leave home, I figured that our good-byes at Clemson would be replete with the sort of bawling and emotionalism that would have the entire campus talking about Kevin and "his family" for months. Actually, everybody held up surprisingly well. We hugged Kevin on the front steps of his dorm, said good-bye, and the rest of the family jumped in the van to head back to Texas. Not a single tear was shed.

It was not until around a hundred miles down the road that a song came over the radio that triggered my emotions, and I started crying. Within seconds, Karen and our three daughters were sobbing, too, and the van was practically rocking with our wailing. I finally pulled over at a roadside convenience store to "towel off." I went inside to get a soda and started weeping again. I tossed my billfold to Karen to pay, and I went back outside to stand by the van. When she came out, we embraced, and I said, "You know, if that boy had been home one more day…I'd have killed him. But I already miss him so!"

That is family, is it not? Loving one another in spite of our imperfections and staying committed to each other and to the relational hope that the family represents.

That evening, we stopped for the night in Louisiana and called Kevin to see how his first day in college had gone. He said, "Did you get my letter? It's in the side pocket of the van's front passenger door." We went out and retrieved the letter. It said:

Dearest Mom and Dad,

Over the past eighteen years, I've led you on a "merry chase," and you have always been there for me. Never once have I doubted that you loved me with all your hearts. I *know* that I am loved by God and by you. That love strengthens me and is a constant source of hope. It may take me a little longer than you'd like for me to get to where you want me to go…and I may not take the exact path you would have me to take…but trust me, I am going to have a wonderful life!

And that is exactly what has happened. Kevin is grown now, with a beautiful family, and he is one of the most wonderful human beings I have ever known.

My experience with Kevin taught me that far more important than giving our kids cars, money, clothing, or education is giving them the unconditional love that allows them to embrace their worth as a child of God. That gift, above all others, will give their lives a sense of joy, hope, and meaning.

It is the primary gift that Jesus would convey—if He had a child.

Kevin and Allison Wilkerson
and their children, Payton, Parker, and Presley

CPSIA information can be obtained at www.ICGtesting.com
Printed in the USA
LVOW01s1535080115

422027LV00018B/1034/P